1974

A MODEST ENQUIRY INTO

THE NATURE OF

WITCHCRAFT

1702

BY

JOHN HALE

FACSIMILE REPRODUCTION

WITH AN INTRODUCTION

BY

RICHARD TRASK, Archivist

Town of Danvers, Massachusetts

Bainbridge, New York

YORK MAIL-PRINT, INC.

1973

YORK MAIL-PRINT, INC.
PRUYN & PARSONS STS.
BAINBRIDGE, NEW YORK
JOHN Y. COMPTON, GENERAL EDITOR

ISBN 0-913126-05-5

Manufactured In The U.S.A.

INTRODUCTION

One of the rarest volumes in the literature of American witchcraft is Reverend John Hale's *A Modest Enquiry Into the Nature of Witchcraft*. This 176-page volume is less known than the contemporary witchcraft writings of Cotton Mather and Robert Calef; and its rarity and limited quotations in print have rather obscured Hale's thesis and findings. Yet, for an understanding of the witchcraft period and one man's explanation of it, the book is of great value. Printed in Boston in 1702, the volume is perhaps the most balanced contemporary account of the Salem Witchcraft period, written by one of the chief participants in the trials. The first printed quotes of the Hale book came from Cotton Mather in his *Magnalia Christi Americana.*[1] Mather quoted 17 pages of the Hale manuscript, not then in print, centering mainly on Hale's account of the beginning of the witch outbreak and the credibility of the testimony of the confessing witches, but only touching upon the so-called "mistaken principles" used in the trials about which Hale wrote at length and was most interested in exposing.

It is not known how many volumes of the 1702 Hale work were printed, but if present-day scarcity of the volume has anything to do with it, the number was not extensive. There appears to have been only one reprint, and this 1771, 158-page Kneeland and Adams, Boston edition is today rarer yet than the 1702 original. In more recent years George Lincoln Burr, in his well-edited 1914 *Narratives of the Witchcraft Cases*, included approximately 62 important pages of the Hale book,[2] but skipped many of the most revealing passages. Most witchcraft scholars have all but ignored the importance of the Hale volume, until recent years when Chadwick Hansen, in his book *Witchcraft at Salem,*[3] found this book to be significant and helpful to his thesis.

The author of *A Modest Enquiry* was born June 3, 1636, in Charlestown, Massachusetts, being the eldest child of Robert and Joanna Hale. Robert Hale was a blacksmith by trade and appears to have come to New England in 1630 as a part of the John Winthrop "Great Migration" fleet. The family took an active role in the ecclesiastical setting up of the new territory, and Robert became one of the first members of the Boston church.

In October, 1632, Robert and his wife helped found the Church at Charlestown, Robert being one of the first two deacons of this congregation. John Hale studied divinity at Harvard and graduated at the age of 21 with the class of 1657. He was admitted to full membership in the Charlestown church the following year.

About this time, some 15 miles to the north of Charlestown, the Church at Salem was being pressured by many of its members living in outlying districts. These people wanted to be spared the long journey to the Salem Church and desired to worship in a meeting house closer to home. One such group lived on the so-called Bass River side of Salem, located to the north of the town, but separated by the Wooleston River and one of its salt water fingers known as Bass River. From as early as 1649 these settlers on the Bass River side had petitioned for a separate church, so in 1656 the Salem Congregation allowed them to build a meetinghouse, but insisted that they would remain legally a part of the mother church.

John Hale was invited, and began preaching at Bass River about 1664. He was offically asked to become pastor in May, 1665. Two years later the inhabitants of Bass River, by then known as Beverly, were given their liberty to set up an independent church with John Hale as its pastor.

To the northwest of Beverly was located Salem Village, another area that had been trying for years to break away from the Salem mother church. When Beverly set up their own congregation, many of the inhabitants of Salem Village found the Beverly church more convenient to attend than the Church at Salem. In 1672 the Salem Villagers received permission to build their own meetinghouse, and by 1689 they became ecclesiastically independent; but the ties with Beverly remained strong, and Rev. Hale continued his friendship with many of the Salem Village inhabitants, including several who would become enmeshed in the witchcraft outbreak in 1692.[4]

On December 15, 1664, Hale married Rebecca, daughter of Henry

Byley, of Salisbury, Massachusetts, and they produced two children, Rebecca, born in 1666, and Robert, born in 1668. In April of 1683 Mrs. Hale died at the age of 45, and on March 31, 1684, Hale married Sarah Noyes, a minister's daughter. This marriage produced three sons and a daughter.

In 1690, Rev. Hale was invited to be a chaplain in the William Phips military expedition against Canada and accepted, much to the displeasure of his congregation. Hale served from June 4 to November 20, acting not only as chaplain to the men, but also as a military interpreter. During his absence from Beverly, his son Robert served as preacher.

Rev. Hale's knowledge of incidents involving suspected witchcraft predated the 1692 Salem Village outbreak by some 44 years. In 1648 Margaret Jones of Charlestown was the first person in New England to be accused and executed for being a witch. Hale, who knew of Jones, was then a lad of 12 years living in Charlestown; and he recounts in his 1702 book that "The day of her Execution, I went in company of some Neighbours, who took great pains to bring her to confession & repentance" (p. 17). According to Hale, Jones was adamant that she was not a witch "and so she said unto her Death" (p.17).

Another incident relating to witchcraft occurred during Hale's pastorate at Beverly. About 1687 Rev. Hale was asked by Christian Trask, a member of his congregation, to disallow Bridget Bishop from receiving the Lord's Supper due to Bishop's keeping an ordinary in her house wherein much drinking and game playing took place. The night following her visit to Hale, Trask became distracted, as Hale later reported, with symptoms like those of the afflicted at Salem Village in 1692. Her distraction seemed to come and go for a month's time, and during one period of recovery Trask claimed that she had been bewitched by Bridget Bishop. Bishop had a reputation along these lines, and had even been brought to the Court of Assistants in 1680 on suspicion of practicing witchcraft, but had been released. Hale appeared troubled at this possibility, though he seems to have rejected the idea "hopeing better of said Goody Bishop."

Subsequently Trask seemed to have made friends with Bishop. Then, under another distraction she suddenly killed herself with a pair of scissors jabbed to the neck. Hale stated in a deposition on May 20, 1692, during Bridget Bishop's witchcraft trial ". . . I then judged and still do apprehend it impossible for her with so short a pair of scissors to mangle herself so without some extraordinary work of the devil or witchcraft." and he did not rule out her distraction as having been caused by bewitchment.[5] But in 1687 neither Hale, nor anyone else did anything about their suspicions.

When the witchcraft panic first broke out in the Rev. Samuel Parris' house in Salem Village, Hale and other neighboring ministers went there to pray and enquire into the sufferings of the afflicted girls. Concerning the afflicted children, Hale relates "Sometimes they were taken dumb, their mouths stopped, their throats choaked, their limbs wracked and tormented so as might move an heart of stone, to sympathize with them" (p. 24). As for their malady, the ministers concluded ". . . they were preternatural, and feared the hand of Satan was in them" (p. 25).

When the afflicted girls began naming their afflictors, and as the accusations grew, those ministers in the immediate area could not help but get immersed in the proceedings. Four of Rev. Hale's parishioners were accused during the eight-month period when the witchcraft panic was at its height. Hale knew Job Tookey, Sarah Merill, Susanna Roote, and Dorcas Hoar of Beverly, and during the trial of Hoar, he swore to a lengthy deposition concerning Goody Hoar. According to the deposition, Hale claimed that there were stories circulated some years ago that Hoar was a fortune teller. He stated that 22 years ago Hoar had confessed to him her evil life and her possession of a book of palmistry, and that she had seemed to renounce all such practices. Then, in 1678, Hale learned that a servant of his and the Hoar children were stealing goods from his house. Although Hale's daughter, Rebecca, knew of the stealing, she was afraid to say anything. Rebecca had been told that Goody Hoar was a witch who knew what Rebecca did and that if Rebecca told on the culprits, Hoar would raise the devil to kill her. Rebecca also reported that she had seen a book that Hoar owned by which she worked witchcraft. In the same deposition Hale stated that he had gone to the jail at Boston to speak with Hoar, who gave explanations to many of his questions. As a whole the Hale deposition seemed to carry no malice in it, and reported facts about Hoar that he had heard from both sides.[6]

That Hale was firmly convinced of the existence of witchcraft in the Salem Village area in 1692 cannot be denied. During the first half dozen months of the witchcraft outbreak there was too much evidence in favor of it for him not to believe. Hale was often in the midst of the proceedings, he was present at many of the examinations and trials, he personally knew many of the afflicted and the accused, and he spent much of his time in the jails praying with or for, and examining the accused and condemned. Looking back five years later, Hale described the horrible condition of the afflicted, and reiterated the credibility of the confession of Tituba, Rev. Samuel Parris' slave who was one of the first three to be arrested. According to Hale, Tituba had all the earmarks of a true penitent witch. Her story was always consistent, she was extremely penitent for her sins, and after her confession she became a sufferer. Hale pointed out that ". . . the success of *Tituba's* confession encouraged those in Authority to examine others that were suspected, and the event was, that more confessed themselves guilty of the Crimes they were suspected for. And thus was this matter driven on" (p. 27). Thus it was that the numerous complaints and sufferings of the afflicted and the over fifty confessions of the accused kept the proceedings going.

Just when Hale first became suspicious of the proceedings is not known, although some early writers believe he was one of the first. There is some evidence that he was seriously doubting the proceedings by August 1692. In November 1692, rumors began to circulate that Hale's pregnant wife, Sarah, was about to be accused. Some speculate that this accusation was coming about, due to Hale's expressing doubts concerning the proceedings. Apparently this factor was the final proof for Hale that the proceedings had gone too far. Writing in 1697, Hale noted that the large number of accused, and the quality of some of the accused persons, indicated better things of them. The fact that the number of afflicted was ever increasing, and that of the 19 hanged witches, all had denied their guilt and some had lived blameless lives before the witchcraft period, reinforced his conclusion that the witchcraft trials had proceeded too far.

When Hale first decided to write his book is unknown. He does inform the reader in the preface that he thought it necessary that someone collect a summary of the witchcraft procedures ". . . which might at least give some light to them which come after, to shun the Rocks by which we were bruised, and narrowly escaped Shipwrack upon. And I have waited five years for some other person to undertake it, who might doe it better than I can, but find none; and judge it better to do what I can, than that such a work should be left undone. Better sincerely though weakly done, then not at all . . ." (pp. 9 & 10).

Samuel Sewall, the diarist and witchcraft judge noted in his diary entry for November 19, 1697, "Mr. Hale and I lodg'd together; He discours'd me about writing a History of the Witchcraft; I fear lest he go into the other extream."[7] Sewall, however, had nothing to fear from the pen of Rev. Hale. The preface to the volume was finished by Hale on December 15, 1697, and Rev. Higginson, pastor at Salem, signed his epistle to the reader March 23, 1697/8. The book was not printed by Green and Allen of Boston, however, until 1702, two years after the death of John Hale; perhaps abiding by the author's wish.

Sarah Hale died May 20, 1695, at the age of 41, and on August 8, 1698, Hale married his third wife, Elizabeth, the widow of Nathaniel Clark. After a pastorate in Beverly of 47 years, Rev. Hale died May 15, 1700. His grave lies near the site of his church and beside the graves of his first two wives. The inscription on the slate stone reads: "Here lyes the body of the Reverend Mr. John Hale a pious and faithfull minister of the gospel and pastor of the first Gather'd Church of Christ in this towne of Beverly, who rest'd from his labours on the 15th day of May anno domini 1700 in the 64th year of his age."[8]

A Modest Enquiry Into the Nature of Witchcraft, and How Persons Guilty of that Crime may be Convicted: And the means used for their Discovery Discussed, both Negatively and Affirmatively, according to SCRIPTURE and EXPERIENCE was the full title of the Hale book, and it synopsized the main points of the volume. Hale appears to have been personally uneasy with the overwhelming scope of his theme, and cognizant of his own inadequacies. He feared lest his book would be taken as an attack on the idea of puritan consensus, the belief in witchcraft, or the beliefs of the puritan forefathers. Thus Hale states that "The middle way is commonly the way of truth." (p. 11) and admits to have taken pains to prove the reality of witchcraft. Hale's guarded reserve often appears to get in the way of his main theme; yet allowing for his position and the fears of the ruling class concerning extremes, his book is a thoughtful, perhaps heart-wracking work that Hale believed was necessary no matter how weak the instrument of its thesis. The Bible was his reference book of truth, and he made no statement contradicting prevalent beliefs without personal experience and scriptural passages ready to back him up. One might wish Hale had carried his thesis further and made it clearer, but realizing the circumstances of the times and the writer, his book is remarkable enough.

The volume is prefaced by an epistle to the reader written by the venerable 82-year-old pastor of the church at Salem, John Higginson, who due to his advanced age had little to do with the witchcraft trials, and was free from their stigma. After giving reasons why the Hale book was useful and needful, Higginson recommended the work written in a ". . . pious and modest manner . . ." to be ". . . generally acceptable to all the lovers of Truth and Peace" (p. 5).

With this Higginson "Imprimatur" on the book, Hale then prefaced the text by explaining the difficulty of the witchcraft theme and his apologetic reasons for writing it. Concerning the traditional methods of finding witches, Hale declared: "I have been from my Youth trained up in the knowledge and belief of most of those principles I here question as unsafe to be used. . . . . . . the reverence I bore to aged, learned and judicious persons, caused me to drink in their principles in these things, with a kind of Implicit Faith.... .... But observing the Events of that sad Catastrophe, *Anno* 1692. I was brought to a more strict scanning of the principles I had imbibed, and by scanning, to question, and by questioning at length to reject many of them, upon the reasons shewed in the ensuing Discourse" (pp. 10 & 11).

The initial chapter of the book defined for the reader who the Devil was, and went into a brief history of the New England witchcraft cases from 1646 to 1692. Chapters II and III centered around the story of the beginning of the Salem Village witchcraft, Tituba's confession and the confession of the other witches, as well as how the trials came to an abrupt end. In Chapter IV Hale wrote concerning indications of why the proceedings had gone too far, and how mistaken principles of evidence had been the chief culprit. Beginning in Chapter V, Hale explained what the traditional principles of common law and practices regarding the discovery of witches were and how they were unreliable in the light of experience and the scriptures. Hale indicated that many of the so-called traditional proofs of witchcraft probably stemmed from common misconceptions of natural phenomena, fantasies, imaginations, or delusions, and that many persons attributed to Satan powers that he did not possess.

One of the most interesting of Hale's observations centered around how Satan used the incorrect beliefs of individuals about witchcraft to ensnarl others. During the witch examinations an experiment was performed on some so-called image articles that Candy, a slave who confessed to being a witch, claimed were used by her to afflict others. One of these images, a piece of rag, was taken by an examiner and burned, whereupon the afflicted girls screamed that they had been burned on the hand. Another piece of the rag was submerged in water, and others of the afflicted acted as if they were choking under water. Hale says of this: "Here note, that the raggs on which, as the Confessor said, the Witchcraft was laid, did when put into fire and water, affect the persons supposed to be thereby bewitched more than the Charmer her self" (p. 81). In other words, it was not the witch performing the afflictions with the images, but the manipulation of the image articles by others which seemed to cause the affliction. If this were so and the witch did not do the afflicting, then from whence did the afflicting come? From the innocent examiners?

Hale explains, "And probably the cause may be, that Satan, the Lord permitting him, may inflict his mischief on the person, the Spectators or Actors herein suppose to be concerned, suiting hereby his design to mans faith about it" (p. 81). Thus it was Satan and not the accused witch or the manipulation of the articles by others who afflicted the girls. Satan used the spectators' own beliefs that if an affliction took place by manipulating the accused witch's image articles, it would prove the witch's guilt. Satan was making occur exactly what the examiners expected, except that they mistakenly attributed the afflicting to the accused witch who could not perform image witchcraft without doing it herself. Thus the accused witch was proven guilty even though in Hale's mind this only proved that Satan took advantage of any situation to bring about evil.

Hale concludes: "And if so, the reason why any suspected person is hereby concerned, is not because they are guilty, but because they are suspect" (p. 81). Thus Hale saw the horror in the proceedings. Satan would use all means possible to prove a person a witch when the person was accused, relying on his own devious powers and man's ill-founded faith about witchcraft to make the innocent look guilty. Therefore, no one was safe while the mistaken principles of discovering a witch were being used, and Satan would take full advantage of the circumstances. This brought a different light upon the proceedings, and pointed out that even the most sincere and righteous of persons could be deadly mistaken.[9]

Among the traditional means used to discover a witch that Hale rejected as dangerous principles to use were the beliefs (1) That Satan cannot assume the shape of innocent persons; (2) That the devil harms persons only with the help of our neighbors; (3) That the witch's casting of an eye upon afflicted persons would send them into terrible fits; (4) That afflicted persons would come out of their misery if touched by a witch; (5) That binding a witch with chains would prevent her from afflicting others; (6) That devil marks on a person's body was evidence of guilt; (7) That the testimony of ghosts to afflicted persons should be relied upon; (8) That persons confessing to be witches is positive proof of guilt.

In Chapters XIII through XVII Hale went into the definition of what a witch is and the differences between the so-called white and black witchcrafts with examples and scriptural proofs. Chapter XVII warned against going to the other extreme of disbelief in the reality of witchcraft with examples of how others had fallen into that trap after the Salem Village proceedings. In this chapter is also discussed how to discover who is a witch and how it should be done properly.

In the concluding chapter Hale made some important observations. It was quite apparent to him that much innocent blood had been shed in the Christian world by condemning with the use of unsafe principles. Continuing in this vein, he stated: "But I would come yet nerer to our own times, and bewail the errors and mistakes that have been in the year 1692. In the apprehending too many we may believe were innocent, and executing of some, I fear, not to have been condemned; by following such traditions of our fathers, maxims of the Common Law, and Presidents and Principles, which now we may see weighed in the balance of the Sanctuary, are found too light. . . . . . . I am abundantly satisfyed that those who were most concerned to act and judge in those matters, did not willingly depart from the rules of righteousness. But such was the darkness of that day, the tortures and lamentations of the afflicted, and the power of former presidents, that we walked in the clouds, and could not see our way" (p. 167). After calling for clearing the names of those innocent witch victims, Hale said: "In the prosecution of Witchcraft, we sought not the Lord after the due order; but have proceeded after the methods used in former times and other places, until the Lord in this tremendous way made a breach upon us. And hereby we are made sensible that the methods formerly used are not sufficient to prove the guilt of such a crime. And this I conceive was one end of the Lord's letting Satan loose to torment and accuse so many; that hereby we may search out the truth more exactly. For had it not been for this dreadful dispensation, many would have lived and dyed in that error, which they are now convinced of" (p. 172).

Thus, to Reverend Hale, the whole horrible Salem Village witch period was due to the people's not heeding the scriptures of God and instead proceeding along with unsafe and unorthodox methods of discovering witches; and that good in the form of a realization of their error and their escape from making the same mistake in the future had come from this near catastrophe.

After committing to paper his long thought out conclusions concerning the Salem Village witchcraft proceedings, Hale ended the manuscript with typical ministerial invocation asking the Lord not to leave nor forsake His people. Hale's conscience must have sighed with relief once the work was completed, though he could never know the reaction of the public to his efforts.

Danvers Archival Center   Richard B. Trask
Danvers, Massachusetts
January 22, 1973

NOTES

1   Cotton Mather, *Magnalia Christi Americana* 2 vols., ed. Thomas Robbins (Hartford, Conn., 1853-1855), II, pp. 471-479.

2   George Lincoln Burr, *Narratives of the Witchcraft Cases, 1648-1706* (New York, 1914), pp. 397-432.

3   Chadwick Hansen, *Witchcraft at Salem* (New York, 1969), pp. 200-202.

4   It was in Salem Village, and not Salem, that the witchcraft panic began and where most of the chief participants of the trials lived. Salem Village was first settled about 1636. In 1752 it became a district, and in 1757 the Town of Danvers, Massachusetts.

5   *John Hale vs. Bridget Bishop*, May 20, 1692. The original deposition is located at the Essex County Court House in Salem. Copies of this and all other official documents from over eight scattered resource centers, may be found in the three volume typescript set, *Salem Witchcraft,* compiled as a W.P.A. project in 1938. This set is perhaps the most important single source on Salem Village Witchcraft. Copies of the set may be found in the Essex Institute of Salem and the Danvers, Massachusetts, Archival Center which houses the most extensive collection of printed material relating to the Salem Village Witchcraft.

6   *John Hale vs. Dorcas Hoar,* July 6, 1692. The original deposition is located in the Essex County Court House, Salem, Massachusetts. A copy may be found in the W.P.A. work, *Salem Witchcraft.*

7   Samuel Sewall, *Diary of Samuel Sewall,* 3 vols. in the *Collections of the Massachusetts Historical Society,* 5th ser., V (Boston, 1878), 464.

8   A more complete biography of John Hale may be found in J. L. Sibley's *Biographical Sketches of Harvard University*, 4 vols. (Cambridge, Mass., 1873) I, pp. 509-520, and in the *Collections of the Massachusetts Historical Society*, 3rd ser., VII, pp. 255-269.

9   Hansen, pp. 200-201.

A Modeſt Enquiry

Into the Nature of

Witchcraft,

AND

How Perſons Guilty of that Crime may be *Convicted* : And the means uſed for their Diſcovery Diſcuſſed, both *Negatively* and *Affirmatively*, according to *SCRIPTURE* and *EXPERIENCE.*

By John Hale,

Paſtor of the Church of Chriſt in *Beverley,*
Anno Domini. 1 6 9 7.

When they ſay unto you, ſeek unto them that have Familiar Spirits and unto Wizzards, that peep,&c. To the Law and to the Teſtimony ; if they ſpeak not according to this word, it is becauſe there is no light in them, Iſaiah VIII. 19, 20.
That which I ſee not teach thou me, Job 34 32.

BOSTON in N. E.
Printed by *B. Green,* and *J. Allen,* for *Benjamin Eliot* under the Town Houſe. 1702

Any general Custom against the Law of God is void. *St. Germans Abridgment of Common Law.* Lib. 1. C. 6.

Omnium legum est inanis censura nisi Divinæ legis imaginem gerat. Finch of Common Law. Lib. 4. C. 3.

Where a Law is grounded upon a Presumption, if the Presumption fail the Law is not to be holden in Conscience. *Abridgment of C. Law.* Lib. 1. C. 19.

An Epiſtle to the
READER.

IT hath been ſaid of Old, That Time is the Mother of Truth, and Truth is the Daughter of Time. It is the Prerogative of the God of Truth, to know all the truth in all things at once and together : It is alſo his Glory to conceal a matter, Prov 25. 2. And to bring the truth to light in that manner and meaſure, and the times appointed, as it pleaſeth him; it is our duty in all humility, and with fear and trembling to ſearch after truth, knowing that ſecret things belong to God, and only things revealed belong to us, and ſo far as they are revealed; for in many things it may be ſaid, what God is doing we know not now; but we, or others that ſucceed us, ſhall know hereafter. Omitting other Examples, I ſhall Inſtance only in the matter of Witchcraft, which on the Humane ſide, is one of the moſt hidden Works of Darkneſs, managed by the Rulers of the darkneſs of this World, to the doing of great ſpoil amongſt the Children of men : And on the Divine ſide, it is one of the moſt awful and tremendous

Judgments

Judgments of God which can be inflicted on the Societies of men, especially when the Lord shall please for his own Holy Ends to Enlarge Satans Commmission in more than an ordinary way.

It is known to all men, that it pleased God some few years ago, to suffer Satan to raise much trouble amongst us in that respect, the biginning of which was very small, and looked on at first as an ordinary case which had fallen out before at several times in other places, & would be quickly over. Only one or two persons belonging to Salem Village about five miles from the Town being suspected, were Examined, &c. But in the progress of the matter, a multitude of other persons both in that and other Neighbour Towns, were Accused, Examined, Imprisoned, and came to their Trials, at Salem, the County Town, where about Twenty of them Suffered as Witches; and many others in danger of the same Tragical End : and still the number of the Accused increased unto many Scores ; amongst whom were many Persons of unquestionable Credit, never under any grounds of suspicion of that or any other Scandalous Evil. This brought a general Consternation upon all sorts of People, doubting what would be the issue of such a dreadful Judgment of God upon the Country ; but the Lord was pleased suddenly to put a stop to those proceedings, that there was no further trouble, as hath been related by others. But it left in the minds of men a sad remembrance of that sorrowful time; and a Doubt whether some Innocent Persons might not Suffer.

Suffer, and ſome guilty Perſons Eſcape. There is no doubt but the Judges and Juries proceeded in their Integrity, with a zeal of God againſt Sin, according to their beſt light, and according to Law and Evidence; but there is a Queſtion yet unreſolved, Whether ſome of the Laws, Cuſtoms and Principles uſed by the Judges and Juries in the Trials of Witches in England (which were followed as Patterns here) were not inſufficient and unſafe.

As for my Self, being under the Infirmities of a decrepit Old Age, I ſtirred little abroad, and was much diſenabled (both in body and mind) from knowing and judging of Occurrents and Tranſactions of that time: But my Reverend Brother Mr. Hale, having for above Thirty Years, been Paſtor of the Church at Beverly (but Two Miles from Salem, where the Tryals were) was frequently preſent, and was a diligent Obſerver of all that paſſed, and being one of a Singular Prudence and Sagacity, in ſearching into the narrows of things: He hath (after much deliberation) in this Treatiſe, related the Subſtance of the Caſe as it was, and given Reaſons from Scripture againſt ſome of the Principles & Practiſes then uſed in the Tryals of Witchcraft; and ſaid ſomething alſo in a Poſitive way, and ſhewing the right Application that is to be made of the whole, and all this in ſuch a pious and modeſt manner, as cannot be offenſive to any, but may be generally acceptable to all the lovers of Truth and Peace.

I

I am the more willing to accompany him to the *Preſs, becauſe I am perſwaded ſuch a Treatiſe as* *this is needful & uſeful upon divers accounts*   As,

1. *That the Works of God may be known ; and* *that God may be more acknowledged and adored, in* *his Juſtice, and in his Mercy: in his Juſtice by* *letting looſe Evil Angels, to make ſo great a ſpoyl* *amongſt us as they did, for the Puniſhment of a de-* *clining People : And in his Mercy, by Countermand-* *ing of Satans Commiſſion, and keeping of him in* *Chains of reſtraint, that he ſhould proceed no fur-* *ther.* Pſal. 83. laſt.

2. *That the Truth of things may be more fully* *known, ſo far as God ſhall pleaſe to reveal the ſame* *in the uſe of lawful means ; for the Judgments of* *God are a great deep, and he is wont to make* *known truth by degrees : and Experience teacheth* *us, there is need of more to be ſaid than hath been* *yet, for the clearing up of difficulties about the mat-* *ter of* Witchcraft. *We ought to be fellow helpers* *to the truth.* 3 Epiſtle of John 8. v.

3. *That whatever Errors or Miſtakes we fell* *into, in the dark hour of Temptation that was upon* *us, may be (upon more light) ſo diſcovered, ac-* *knowledged and diſowned by us, as that it may be* *matter of Warning & Caution to thoſe that come* *after us, that they may not fall into the like.* 1 Cor. 10. 11.   Fælix quem faciunt aliena pericula cautum.

4. *And that it may Occaſion the moſt Learned* *and Pious men to make a further & fuller Enquiry* *into*

into the matter of Witchcraft, *eſpecially into the poſitive part, How* Witches *may be ſo diſcovered, that innocent perſons may be preſerved; and none but the guilty may ſuffer.*　Prov. 17. 15

　Verily whoſoever ſhall by the Grace of God be enabled to Contribute further light in this matter, will do good Service to God and Men in his Generation.

　I would alſo propound and leave it as an Object of Conſideration to our Honoured Magiſtrates and Reverend Miniſters, Whether the Æquity of that Law in Leviticus, *Chap. 4. for a Sin offering for the Rulers and for the Congregation, in the caſe of Sins of Ignorance, when they come to be known, be not Obliging, and for direction to us in a Goſpel way.*

　Now the Father of Lights & Mercies grant unto us, that Mercy & Truth may meet together, that righteouſneſs and peace may kiſs each other, that the Glory of God may dwell in our Land; and that it may be ſaid of New-England, *The Lord Bleſs thee, O Habitation of Juſtice & Mountain of Holineſs.*

　Finally, That the Bleſſing of Heaven may go along with this little Treatiſe to attain the good Ends thereof, is, and ſhall be the Prayer of him who is daily waiting for his Change, and looking for the Mercy of the Lord Jeſus Chriſt *unto Eternal Life.*

John Higginſon,
Paſtor of the Church,
of *Salem.*
Ætatis 82.

March 23d.
1697, 8.

The

[8]

The Preface

TO THE

Christian READER.

THE Holy Scriptures inform us that the Doctrine of Godliness is a great Mystery, containing the Mysteries of the Kingdom of Heaven : Mysteries which require great search for the finding out : And as the Lord hath his Mysteries to bring us to Eternal Glory ; so Satan hath his Mysteries to bring us to Eternal Ruine : Mysteries not easily understood, whereby the depths of Satan are managed in hidden wayes. So the Whore of *Babylon* makes the *Inhabitants of the Earth drunk with the Wine of her Fornication*, by the Mystery of her abominations, *Rev.* 17. 2. And the man of Sin hath his Mystery of iniquity whereby he deceiveth men through the working of Satan in signes and lying wonders, 2 *Thes.* 2 3, 7, 9.

And among Satans Mysteries of iniquity, this of *Witchcraft* is one of the most difficult to be searched out by the Sons of men ; as appeareth

by

by the great endeavours of Learned and Holy men to search it out, and the great differences that are found among them, in the rules laid down for the bringing to light these hidden works of darkness. So that it may seem presumption in me to undertake so difficult a *Theam*, & to lay down such rules as are different from the Sentiments of many Eminent writers, and from the Presidents and practices of able Lawyers ; yea and from the Common Law it self.

But my Apology for this undertaking is ;

1. That there hath been such a dark dispensation by the Lord, letting loose upon us the Devil, *Anno.* 1691. & 1692. as we never experienced before : And thereupon apprehending and condemning persons for *Witchcraft* ; and nextly acquitting others no less liable to such a charge ; which evidently shew we were in the dark, and knew not what to do ; but have gone too far on the one or other side, if not on both. Hereupon I esteemed it necessary for some person to Collect a Summary of that affair, with some animadversions upon it, which might at least give some light to them which come after, to shun those Rocks by which we were bruised, and narrowly escaped Shipwrack upon. And I have waited five years for some other person to undertake it, who might doe it better than I can, but find none ; and judge it better to do what I can,

than

than that such a work should be left undone. Better sincerely though weakly done, then not at all, or with such a byas of prejudice as will put false glosses upon that which was managed with uprightness of heart, though there was not so great a spirit of discerning, as were to be wished in so weighty a Concernment.

2. I have been present at several Examinations and Tryals, and knew sundry of those that Suffered upon that account in former years, and in this last affair, and so have more advantages than a stranger, to give account of these Proceedings.

3. I have been from my Youth trained up in the knowledge and belief of most of those principles I here question as unsafe to be used. The first person that suffered on this account in *New-England*, about Fifty years since, was my Neighbour, and I heard much of what was charged upon her, and others in those times ; and the reverence I bore to aged, learned and judicious persons, caused me to drink in their principles in these things, with a kind of Implicit Faith. *Quo semel est imbuta recens servabit odorem, Testa diu — A Child will not easily forsake the principles he hath been trained up in from his Cradle.*

But observing the Events of that sad Catastrophe, *Anno* 1692. I was brought to a more strict scanning of the principles I had imbibed, and by scanning, to question, and by questio-

ning

ning at length to reject many of them, upon
the reasons shewed in the ensuing Discourse.
It is an approved saying, *Nihil certius, quam quod
ex dubio fit certum* : No truth more certain to a
man, than that which he hath formerly doubt-
ed or denied, and is recovered from his error,
by the convincing evidence of Scripture & reason. Yet I know and am sensible, that while
we know but in part, man is apt in flying
from a discovered error, to run into the contrary extream.

Incidit in Scyllam qui vult vitare Charybdim.

The middle way is commonly the way of
truth. And if any can shew me a better middle way than I have here laid down, I shall
be ready to embrace it : But the conviction
must not be by vinegar or drollery, but by
strength of argument.

4. I have had a deep sence of the sad con-
sequence of mistakes in matters Capital ; and
their impossibility of recovering when compleated. And what grief of heart it brings to
a tender conscience, to have been unwittingly
encouraging of the Sufferings of the innocent.
And I hope a zeal to prevent for the future
such sufferings is pardonable, although there
should be much weakness, and some errors in
the pursuit thereof.

5. I observe the failings that have been on
the one hand, have driven some into that
which is indeed an extream on the other hand,
and

and of dangerous confequence, *viz.* To deny any fuch perfons to be under the *New-Teftament*, who by the Devils aid difcover Secrets, or do work wonders. Therefore in the latter part of this difcourfe, I have taken pains to prove the Affirmative, yet with brevity, becaufe it hath been done already by *Perkins* of *Witchcraft*. *Glanvil* his *Saducifcus Triumphatus*. Pt. 1. *p*. 1. *to* 90. & Pt. 2. *p* 1 *to* 80. Yet I would not be underftood to juftify all his notions in thofe difcourfes, but acknowledge he hath ftrongly proved the being of *Witches*.

6. I have fpecial reafons moving me to bear my teftimony about thefe matters, *before I go hence & be no more*; the which I have here done, and I hope with fome affiftance of his Spirit to whom I commit my felf & this my labour, even that God *whofe I am & whom I ferve*: Defiring his Mercy in Jefus Chrift to Pardon all the Errors of his People in the day of darknefs; and to enable us to fight with Satan by Spiritual Weapons, putting on the whole Armour of God.

And tho' Satan by his Meffengers may buffet Gods Children, yet there's a promife upon right *Refifting, he fhall flee from them*, Jam. 4. 7. *And that all things fhall work together for the good of thofe that Love the Lord*, Rom. 8. 28. So that I believe Gods Children fhall be gainers by the affaults of Satan, which occafion'd this Difcourfe; which that they may, is the Prayer of Thine in the Service of the Gofpel.

Beverly, Decemb.
15th, 1697.

JOHN HALE

A Modeſt Enquiry,

Into the Nature of

WITCHCRAFT.

CHAPTER I.

Sect. 1. THE Angels who kept not their Firſt Eſtate, by Sin againſt God, loſt their primitive purity, and glorious Excellency, as to their moral qualifications, and became unclean, wicked, envious, lyars, and full of all wickedneſs, which as Spirits they are capable of; Yet I do not find in Scripture that they loſt their natural abilities of underſtanding or power of Operation.

1. As for their Underſtanding, they are called *Daimon* (which we Tranſlate Devil) becauſe they are full of wiſdom, cunning, skill, ſubtilty and knowledge. He hath alſo the name of Serpent from his ſubtilty, 2 *Cor.* 11. 3. And his knowledge in the Scriptures, and

and wittiness to pervert them, appears by his quoting Scripture to our Saviour when he tempted him. *Mat.* 4.

And as there be many Devils, and these active, quick, swift and piercing Spirits, so they going to and fro in the earth, and walking up and down in it, have advantages to know all the actions of the Children of men, both open and secret, their discourses, consultations, and much of the inward affections of men thereby; though still its Gods prerogative immediately to know the heart. *Jer.* 17. 10.

2. As to their natural power as Spirits, its very great, if not equal to that of the Holy Angels : For,

1. They are called *Principalities and Powers. Rom.* 8. 38. *Eph.* 6. 12 *Col.* 2. 14, 15. compared with *Heb.* 2 14, 15. Now these are names given to the Holy Angels. *Eph.* 1. 21. *and* 3. 10.

2. They are called, *Rulers of the darkness of this world, the Prince of the power of the Air. Eph.* 6. 12. *and* 2. 2.

3. Such was their power that they contended with *Michael* and the Angels about the Body of *Moses.* 2 *Pet.* 2. 11. *Jude* 9. That is, as I conceive, about preventing the Burial of the Body of *Moses*: For it's said, *Deut.* 34. 6. The Lord buried him, and no man knoweth of his Sepulcher to this day. That is, he did it by the Ministry of Angels (for the Lord gave the

the Law, *Exod* 20. 1. and that it was by the
Ministry of Angels, see *Gal.* 3. 19. so probably was the burial of *Moses's* Body) and the
Devils endeavour if possible, to discover *Mo-*
ses's Body, or place of its burial, that they
might draw *Israel* to commit Idolatry in worshipping at his Tomb (as our Popish Fore-fa-
thers did at *Thomas Beckets* in *Kent*) from the
Veneration they had to him as their Law giver.

4. The Devils actings against *Job, Chap.* 1.
and 2. and what he did to the *Gadarens* Swine,
&c. Shew his great power. So that we may
conclude, had the Devils liberty to reveal all
that they know of the affairs of mankind, or
to do all that is in their power to perform,
they would bring dreadful confusions and de-
solations upon the World.

Sect. 2. The way God governs Devils is
by Chains. 2 *Pet.* 2. 4. *Jude* 6 *ver. Rev.* 20.
1, 2, 7, 8. whereby they are kept Prisoners.
Men are governed by Laws, by convictions of
Conscience. *Rom.* 2. 12, 13, 14, 15. By Scripture Rules, Humane Laws, and also by Gods
Spirit. 1 *John* 2. 20. But Devils have no such
Laws, or tenderness of Conscience to bridle
or restrain them. But the Lord hath his
Chains, which are called Everlasting, and are
always lasting; so that they are never wholly
without a Chain. This Chain is sometimes
greater and shorter, other times lesser and
longer,

longer, as the Lord pleaseth, for his own Glo-ry, *Rev.* 20. 1, 2, 7, 8 *For as the wrath of man praiseth the Lord, and the remainder of wrath he doth restrain,* *Psal.* 76. 10. So may we say of the Devils wrath.

Sect. 3. The Devil is full of malice against man, and frames his designs against him, chiefly to destroy his Soul, as, 1 *Pet.* 5 8 2 *Cor.* 11. 3. and other Scriptures abundantly testify. Hence probably at sometimes he doth not all the hurt to mans Body that he could, lest thereby he should awaken man to repentance and prayer ; he seeks to keep men in a false peace. *Luk.* 11. 21 Yet at other times he disturbs and afflicts men in Body and Estate ; as Scripture and experience shew. Among the Devi-ces Satan useth to ruine man, one is to allure him into such a familiarity with him, that by Sorceries, Inchantments, Divinations, and such like, he may lead them Captive at his plea-sure. This snare of his we are warned against. *Deut.* 18. 10, 11. and in other Scriptures. This Sin of men hearkening after Satan in these ways, is called Witchcraft ; of which it is my purpose to treat : But first I shall speak some-thing Historically what hath been done in *New England,* in prosecution of persons suspe-cted of this Crime.

Sect. 4. Several persons have been Char-ged

ged with and suffered for the Crime of Witchcraft in the Governments of the *Massachusetts*,
New Haven, or *Stratford* and *Connecticut*, from
the year **1646.** to the year **1692.**

Sect. 5. The first was a Woman of *Charlestown, anno.* 1647. or 48. She was suspected partly
because that after some angry words passing between her & her Neighbours, some mischief be-
fel such Neighbours in their Creatures, or the
like : partly because some things supposed to be
bewitched, or have a Charm upon them, being
burned, she came to the fire and seemed concerned.

The day of her Execution, I went in company of some Neighbours, who took great pains
to bring her to confession & repentance. But
she constantly professed her self innocent of that
crime : Then one prayed her to consider if
God did not bring this punishment upon her
for some other crime, and asked, if she had not
been guilty of Stealing many years ago; she
answered, *she had stolen something, but it was long
since, and she had repented of it, and there was Grace
enough in Christ to pardon that long agoe ; but as
for Witchcraft she was wholly free from it,* and so
she said unto her Death.

Sect. 6. Another that suffered on that account some time after, was a *Dorchester* Woman. And upon the day of her Execution
                    B   Mr.

Mr. _Thompson_ Minister at _Brantry_, and _J. P._ her former Master took pains with her to bring her to repentance And she utterly denyed her guilt of Witchcraft; yet justifyed God for bringing her to that punishment : for she had when a single woman play'd the harlot, and being with Child used means to destroy the fruit of her body to conceal her sin & shame, and although she did not effect it; yet she was a Murderer in the sight of God for her endeavours, and shewed great penitency for that sin; but owned nothing of the crime laid to her charge.

Sect. 7. Another suffering in this kind was a Woman of _Cambridge_, against whom a principal evidence was a _Watertown_ Nurse, who testifyed, that the said _Kendal_ (so was the accused called) did bewitch to Death a Child of Goodman _Genings_ of _Watertown_ ; for the said _Kendal_ did make much of the Child, and then the Child was well, but quickly changed its colour and dyed in a few hours after. The Court took this evidence among others, the said _Genings_ not knowing of it. But after _Kendal_ was Executed (who also denyed her guilt to the Death,) Mr. _Rich Brown_ knowing & hopeing better things of _Kendal_, asked said _Genings_ if they suspected her to bewitch their Child, they answered _No_. But they judged the true cause of the Childs Death to be thus, _viz._ The Nurse had the night before carryed out the Child and

kept

kept it abroad in the Cold a long time, when the red gum was come out upon it, & the Cold had ftruck in the red gum, and this they judged the caufe of the Childs death. And that faid *Kendal* did come in that day and make much of the Child, but they apprehended no wrong to come to the Child by her. After this the faid Nurfe was put into Prifon for Adultery, and there delivered of her bafe Child, and Mr. *Brown* went to her and told her, *It was juft with God to leave her to this wickednefs, as a punifhment for her Murdering goody* Kendal *by her falfe witnefs bearing.* But the Nurfe dyed in Prifon, and fo the matter was not farther inquired into.

There was another Executed, of *Bofton Anno* 1656. for that crime. And two or three of *Springfield,* one of which confeffed ; and faid the occafion of her familiarity with Satan was this : She had loft a Child and was exceedingly difcontented at it, and longed ; *Oh that fhe might fee her Child again !* And at laft the Devil in likenefs of her Child came to her bed fide and talked with her, and asked to come into the bed to her, and fhe received it into the bed to her that night and feveral nights after, and fo entred into covenant with Satan and became a Witch. This was the only confeffor in thefe times in this Government.

Sect. 8, Another at *Hartford,* viz. *Mary*
B 2   *Johnfon,*

Johnson, mentioned in Remarkable Providences, *p.* 62, 63 Confessed her self a Witch. Who upon discontent & slouthfulness agreed with the Devil to do her work for her, and fetch up the Swine. And upon her immoderate laughter at the running of the Swine, as the Devil drove them, as she her self said, was suspected & upon examination confessd. I have also heard of a Girl at *New Haven* or *Stratford*, that confessed her guilt. But all others denyed it unto the death unless one *Greensmith*, at *Hartford*.

Sect. 9. But it is not my purpose to give a full relation of all that have suffered for that Sin, or of all the particulars charged upon them, which probably is now impossible, many witnessing *Viva voce*, those particulars which were not fully recorded. But that I chiefly intend is to shew the principles formerly acted upon in Convicting of that Crime ; which were such as these.

1. The first great principle laid down by a person Eminent for Wisdom, Piety and Learning was ; That the Devil could not assume the shape of an innocent person in doing mischiefs unto mankind : for if the Lord should suffer him in this, he would subvert the course of humane Justice, by bringing men to suffer for what he did in their Shapes.

2. *Witchcraft* being an habitual Crime, one single witness to one Act of Witchcraft, and another

nother single witness to another such fact, made
two witnesses against the Crime and the party
suspected.

3. There was searching of the bodies of the
suspected for such like tears, or spots (which
writers speak of) called the Devils marks ; and if
found, these were accounted a presumption at
least of guilt in those that had them.

4. I observed that people laid great weight
upon this ; when things supposed to be bewitched were burnt, and the suspected person came
to the fire in the time of it.   Although that E-
minent person above said condemned this way
of tryal, as going to the Devil to find the Devil.

5. If after anger between Neighbours mischief followed, this oft bred suspicion of Witchcraft in the matter.   In fine, the presumptions
and convictions used in former times were for
substance the same which we may read of in
Keeble of the Common Law, and in *Bernard*, &
other Authors of that subject.

Sect. 10. About 16 or 17. years since was
accused a Woman of *Newbury*, and upon her
tryal the Jury brought her in Guilty.   Yet the
Governour *Simon Bradstreet* Esq and some of
the Magistrates repreived her, being unsatisfy-
ed in the Verdict upon these grounds.

1. They were not satisfyed that a Specter
doing mischief in her likeness, should be imputed to her person, as a ground of guilt.

2. They

2. They did not eſteem one ſingle witneſs to one fact, and another ſingle witneſs to another fact, for two witneſſes, againſt the perſon in a matter Capital.   She being reprived, was carried to her own home, and her Husband, (who was eſteemed a Sincere and underſtanding Chriſtian by thoſe that knew him) deſired ſome Neighbour Miniſters, of whom I was one, to meet together and diſcourſe his Wife ; the which we did : and her diſcourſe was very Chriſtian among us, and ſtill pleaded her innocence as to that which was laid to her charge. We did not eſteem it prudence for us to paſs any definitive Sentance upon one under her circumſtances, yet we inclined to the more charitable ſide.

In her laſt Sickneſs ſhe was in much darkneſs & trouble of Spirit, which occaſioned a Judicious friend to examine her ſtrictly, Whether ſhe had been guilty of *Witchcraft*, but ſhe ſaid *No* : But the ground of her trouble was ſome impatient & paſſionate Speeches and Actions of hers while in Priſon, upon the account of her ſuffering wrongfully ; whereby ſhe had provoked the Lord, by putting ſome contempt upon his word. And in fine, ſhe ſought her pardon and comfort from God in Chriſt, and dyed ſo far as I underſtood, praying to and reſting upon God in Chriſt for Salvation.

Sect. 11, The next that Suffered was the 7th.

rish Woman of *Boston*, suspected to bewitch
John Goodwins Children, who upon her Tryal
did in *Irish* (as was testified by the Interpreters)
confess her self guilty, and was condemned
out of her own mouth; (as Christ saith, *Luk.*
19.22. *Out of thine own mouth will I Judge thee.*)
The History of which is published by Mr.
Cotton Mather, (and attested by the other Ministers of *Boston* & *Charlstown*,) in his Book, En-
tituled, *Memorable Providences.* Printed *Anno* 1689.
Thus far of the History of Witches before the
year, 1692.

CHAPTER II.

I. IN the latter end of the year 1691. Mr.
Samuel Paris, Pastor of the Church in
Salem-Village, had a Daughter of Nine, and a
Neice of about Eleven years of Age, sadly Afflicted of they knew not what Distempers; and
he made his application to Physitians, yet still
they grew worse : And at length one Physitian gave his opinion, that they were under an
Evil Hand. This the Neighbours quickly took
up, and concluded they were bewitched. He
had also an Indian Man-servant, and his Wife
who afterwards confessed, that without the
knowledge of their Master or Mistress, they
had taken some of the Afflicted persons Urine,
and mixing it with meal had made a Cake,
& baked it, to find out the Witch, as they said.

After this, the Afflicted persons cryed out of
the Indian Woman, named *Tituba*, that she
did pinch, prick, and grievously torment them,
and that they saw her here and there, where
no body else could. Yea they could tell
where she was, and what she did, when out
of their humane sight. These Children were
bitten and pinched by invisible agents; their
arms, necks, and backs turned this way and
that way, and returned back again, so as it was
impossible for them to do of themselves; and
beyond the power of any Epileptick Fits, or
natural Disease to effect. Sometimes they were
taken dumb, their mouths stopped, their throats
choaked, their limbs wracked and tormented
so as might move an heart of stone, to sympathize with them, with bowels of compassion
for them. I will not enlarge in the descripti-
on of their cruel Sufferings, because they
were in all things afflicted as bad as *John Goodwins* Children at *Boston*, in the year 1689. So
that he that will read Mr. *Mathers* Book of
Memorable Providences, page 3. &c. may Read
part of what these Children, and afterwards
sundry grown persons suffered by the hand of
Satan, at *Salem* Village, and parts adjacent,
Anno 1691, 2. Yet there was more in these
Sufferings, than in those at *Boston*, by pins invisibly stuck into their flesh, pricking with I-
rons, (As in part published in a Book Printed
1693. *viz. The Wonders of the Invisible World.*)

Mr.

Mr. *Paris* feeing the diſtreſſed condition of his Family, defired the preſence of fome **Wor**thy Gentlemen of *Salem,* and fome Neighbour Miniſters to confult together at his Houfe ; who when they came, and had enquired diligently into the Sufferings of the Afflicted, concluded they were preternatural, and feared the hand of Satan was in them.

II. The advice given to Mr. *Paris* by them was, that he fhould fit ftill and wait upon the Providence of God to fee what time might difcover ; and to be much in prayer for the difcovery of what was yet fecret. They alfo Examined *Tituba,* who confeffed the making a Cake, as is above mentioned, and faid her Miſtreſs in her own Country was a **Witch,** and had taught her fome means to be uſed for the difcovery of a Witch and for the prevention of being bewitched, &c. But faid that fhe her felf was not a Witch.

III. Soon after this, there were two or three private Faſts at the Miniſters Houfe, one of which was kept by fundry Neighbour Mini-fters, and after this, another in Publick at the *Village,* and feveral days afterwards of publick Humiliation, during thefe moleſtations, not only there, but in other Congregations for them. And one General Faſt by Order of the General Court, obferved throughout the Colony,

Colony to feek the Lord that he would rebuke
Satan, and be a light unto his people in this day
of darknefs.

But I return to the Hiftory of thefe trou-
bles. In a fhort time after other perfons who
were of age to be witneffes, were molefted by
Satan, and in their fits cryed out upon *Tituba*
and Goody O. & S. G. that they or Specters in
their Shapes did grievoufly torment them ;
hereupon fome of their Village Neighbours
complained to the Magiftrates at *Salem*, defiring
they would come and examine the afflicted &
accufed together ; the which they did : the
effect of which examination was, that *Tituba*
confeffed fhe was a Witch, and that fhe with the
two others accufed did torment & bewitch the
complainers, and that thefe with two others
whofe names fhe knew not, had their Witch-
meeting together ; relating the times when &
places where they met, with many other cir-
cumftances to be feen at large. Upon this the
faid *Tituba* and O. & S. G. were committed to
Prifon upon fufpicion of acting Witchcraft.
After this the faid *Tituba* was again examined
in Prifon, and owned her firft confeffion in all
points, and then was her felf afflicted and complained of her fellow Witches tormenting of
her, for her confeffion, and accufing them, and
being fearched by a Woman, fhe was found to
have upon her body the marks of the Devils
wounding of her.

IV.

IV. Here were these things rendred her confession credible. (1) That at his examination she answered every question just as she did at the first.   And it was thought that if she had feigned her confession, she could not have remembred her answers so exactly.   A lyar we say, had need of a good memory, but truth being always consistent with it self is the same to day as it was yesterday.   (2) She seemed very penitent for her Sin in covenanting with the Devil. (3) She became a sufferer her self, & as she said for her confession. (4) Her confession agreed exactly (which was afterwards verified in the other confessors) with the accusations of the afflicted.   Soon after these afflicted persons complained of other persons afflicting of them in their fits, and the number of the afflicted and accused began to increase.   And the success of *Tituba's* confession encouraged those in Authority to examine others that were suspected, and the event was, that more confessed themselves guilty of the Crimes they were suspected for.   And thus was this matter driven on.

V. I observed in the prosecution of these affairs, that there was in the Justices, Judges & others concerned, a conscientious endeavour to do the thing that was right.   And to that end they consulted the Presidents of former times & precepts laid down by Learned Writers about Witch.

Witchcraft. As *Keeble* on the *Common Law*, *Chapt*. Conjuration, (an Author approved by the Twelve Judges of our Nation.) Alſo Sir. *Mathew Hales* tryal of Witches, Printed *Anno* 1682. *Glanvils* Collection of ſundry tryals in *England* & *Ireland*, in the years 1658, 61, 63, 64, & 81. *Bernards* guide to Jurymen, *Baxter* & *R. Burton*, their Hiſtories about Witches and their diſcoveries. *Cotton Mather's* Memorable Providences relating to Witchcrafts, Printed *Anno* 1689.

VI. But that which chiefly carried on this matter to ſuch an height, was the increaſing of confeſſors till they amounted to near about Fifty : and four or ſix of them upon their try- als owned their guilt of this crime, and were condemned for the ſame, but not Executed. And many of the confeſſors confirmed their confeſſions with very ſtrong circumſtances : As their exact agreement with the accuſations of the afflicted ; their punctual agreement with their fellow conteſſors ; their relating the times when they covenanted with Satan, and the rea- ſons that moved them thereunto ; their Witch meetings, and that they had their mock Sacra- ments of Baptiſm and the Supper, in ſome of them ; their ſigning the Devils book ; and ſome ſhewed the Scars of the wounds which they ſaid were made to fetch blood with, to ſign the Devils book ; and ſome ſaid they had

Imps.

Imps to fuck them, and fhewed Sores raw where they faid they were fucked by them.

VII. I fhall give the Reader a taft of thefe things in a few Inftances. The Afflicted complained that the Spectres which vexed them, urged them to fet their Hands to a Book reprefented to them (as to them it feemed) with threatnings of great torments, if they figned not, and promifes of eafe if they obeyed.

Among thefe *D. H.* did as fhe faid (which fundry others confeffed afterwards) being overcome by the extremity of her pains, fign the Book prefented, and had the promifed eafe; and immediately upon it a Spectre in her Shape afflicted another perfon, and faid, I have figned the Book and have eafe, now do you fign, and fo fhall you have eafe. And one day this afflicted perfon pointed at a certain place in the room, and faid, there is *D. H.* upon which a man with his Rapier ftruck at the place, though he faw no Shape ; and the Afflicted called out, faying, you have wounded her fide, and foon after the afflicted perfon pointed at another place, faying, there fhe is ; whereupon a man ftruck at the place, and the afflicted faid, you have given her a fmall prick about the eye. Soon after this, the faid *D. H.* confeffed her felf to be made a Witch by figning the Devils Book as above faid ; and declared

that

that she had afflicted the Maid that complained of her, and in doing of it had received two wounds by a Sword or Rapier, a small one about the eye which she shewed to the Magistrates, and a bigger on the side of which she was searched by a discreet woman, who reported, that *D. H* had on her side the sign of a wound newly healed.

This *D H* confess'd that she was at a Witch Meeting at *Salem Village*, where were many persons that she named, some of whom were in Prison then or soon after upon suspicion of Witchcraft: And the said *G. B* preached to them, and such a Woman was their Deacon, and there they had a Sacrament.

VIII. Several others after this confessed the same things with *D H*. In particular Goody *F* said (*Inter alia*) that she with two others (one of whom acknowledged the same) Rode from *Andover* to the same Village Witch meeting upon a stick above ground, and that in the way the stick brake, and gave the said *F.* a fall: whereupon, said she, I got a fall & hurt of which I am still sore. I happened to be present in Prison when this *F.* owned again her former confession to the Magistrates. And then I moved she might be further questioned about some particulars: It was answered, the Magistrates had not time to stay longer; but I should have liberty to Examine her farther

ther by my felf; The which thing I did; and
I asked her if fhe rode to the Meeting on a
Stick; fhe faid, yea.   I enquired what fhe did
for Victuals; fhe anfwered, that fhe carried
Bread and Cheefe in her pocket, and that fhe
and the *Andover* Company came to the Village
before the Meeting began, and fat down together under a tree and eat their food, and that
fhe drank water out of a Brook to quench
her thirft.   And that the Meeting was upon
a plain graffy place, by which was a Cart path,
and fandy ground in the path, in which were
the tracks of Horfes feet.   And fhe alfo told
me how long they were going and returning.
And fome time after told me, fhe had fome
trouble upon her fpirit, and when I enquired
what? fhe faid, fhe was in fear that G. B. and
M. C. would kill her; for they appeared unto
her (in Spectre, for their perfons were kept
in other Rooms in the Prifon) and brought a
fharp pointed iron like a fpindle, but four
fquare, and threatned to ftab her to death
with it; becaufe fhe had confeffed her Witchcraft, and told of them, that they were with
her, and that M. C. above-named was the perfon that made her a Witch.   About a month
after the faid F. took occafion to tell me the
fame Story of her fears that G. B. and M. C.
would kill her, and that the thing was much
upon her Spirits.

IX.

IX. It was not long before *M. L.* Daughter of said *F.* confess'd that she rode with her Mother to the said Witch Meeting, and confirmed the substance of her Mothers Confession. At another time, *M L* junior the Grand Daughter, aged about seventeen years, confesseth the substance of what her Grand mother and Mother had related, and declareth, that when they, with *E. C.* rode on a stick or pole in the Air, She the said Grand-Daughter with *R C.* Rode upon another ; (and the said *R. C.* acknowledged the same) and that they sat their hands to the Devil's Book. And (*inter alia*) said, *O Mother, why did you give me to the Devil?* twice or thrice over. The Mother said, she was sorry at the heart for it, it was through that wicked one. Her Daughter bid her repent and call upon God : And said, *Oh Mother, your wishes are now come to pass ! for how often have you wished that the Devil would fetch me away alive?* And then said, *Oh! my heart will break within me* ; Then she wept bitterly, crying out, *O Lord comfort me, and bring out all the Witches* And she said to her Grandmother, *O Grandmother, why did you give me to the Devil? Why did you perswade me, O Grandmother do not deny it* Then the Grandmother gave account of several things about their confederates and acts of Witchcrafts, too long to rehearse.

CHAP.

CHAPTER III.

NExtly I will insert the Confession of a man about Forty years of Age, *W. B.* which he wrote himself in Prison, and sent to the Magistrates, to confirm his former Confession to them, *viz God having called me to Confess my sin and Apostasy in that fall in giving the Devil advantage over me, appearing to me like a Black, in the evening to set my hand to his Book, as I have owned to my shame: He told me that I should not want so doing. At* Salem Village, *there being a little off the Meeting-House, about and hundred five Blades, some with Rapiers by their side, which was called and might be more for ought I know by* B. *and* Bu. *and the Trumpet sounded, and Bread and Wine which they called the Sacrament, but I had none; being carried over all on a Stick, never being at any other Meeting. I being at Cart a Saturday last, all the day, of Hay and English Corn, the Devil brought my Shape to* Salem, *and did afflict* M. S. *and* R. F. *by clitching my hand; and a Sabbath day my Shape afflicted* A. M. *and at night afflicted* M S. *and* A. M. E. I. *and* A. F. *have been my Enticers to this great abomination, as one have owned and charged her to her Sister with the same. And the design was to destroy* Salem Village, *and to begin at the Minister's House, and to destroy the Church of God, and to set up* Satans *Kingdom, and then all will be well.*

C　　　　　　　　　　　*And*

And now I hope God in some measure has made me something sensible of my sin and apostasy, begging pardon of God, and of the Honourable Magistrates and all Gods people, hoping and promising by the help of God, to set to my heart and hand to do what is me lyeth to destroy such wicked worship, humbly begging the prayers of all Gods People for me, I may walk humbly under this great affliction, and that I may procure to my self, the sure mercies of David, and the blessing of Abraham. Concerning this Confession. (1) Note it was his own free Act in Prison. (2) He saith the Devil like a Black] This he had before explained to be like a Black man (3) That on a certain day was heard in the Air the sound of a Trumpet, at Salem Village nigh the Meeting-House, and upon all enquiry it could not be found that any mortal man did sound it. (4) The three persons he saith the Devil in his Shape afflicted, had been as to the times and manner afflicted as he confesseth. (5) That E. I. confessed as much as W. B. chargeth her with. (6) Many others confessed a Witch Meeting, or Witch meetings at the Village as well as he.

Note also that these Confessors did not only witness against themselves, but against one another; and against many if not all those that Suffered for that Crime. As for example, when G. B. was Tryed, seven or eight of these Confessors severally called, said, they knew the said B. and saw him at a Witch-Meeting

at

at the Village, and heard him exhort the Company to pull down the Kingdom of God, and
set up the Kingdom of the Devil. He denied
all, yet said he justified the Judges and Jury in
Condemning of him ; because there were so
many positive witnesses against him : But said
he dyed by false Witnesses. I seriously spake
to one that witnessed (of his Exhorting at the
Witch Meeting at the Village) saying to her ;
you are one that bring this man to Death, if
you have charged any thing upon him that is
not true, recal it before it be too late, while
he is alive. She answered me, she had nothing to charge her self with, upon that account.

M. C. had to witness against her, two or
three of her own Children, and several of
her Neighbours that said they were in confederacy with her in their Witchcraft.

A. F. Had three of her Children, and some
of the Neighbours, her own Sister, and a Servant, who confessed themselves Witches, and
said, she was in confederacy with them. But
alas, I am weary with relating particulars ;
those that would see more of this kind, let
them have recourse to the Records.

By these things you see how this matter
was carried on, *viz.* chiefly by the complaints
and accusations of the Afflicted, Bewitched
ones, as it was supposed, and then by the Confessions of the Accused, condemning them-

selves,

selves, and others. Yet experience shewed, that the more there were apprehended, the more were still Afflicted by Satan, and the number of Confessors increasing, did but increase the number of the Accused, and the Executing some, made way for the apprehending of others; for still the Afflicted complained of being tormented by new objects, as the former were removed. So that those that were concerned, grew amazed at the numbers and quality of the persons accused, and feared that Satan by his wiles had inwrapped innocent persons under the imputation of that Crime. And at last it was evidently seen that there must be a stop put, or the Generation of the Children of God would fall under that condemnation.

Henceforth therefore the Juries generally acquitted such as were Tried, fearing they had gone too far before. And Sir *William Phips*, Governour, Reprieved all that were Condemned, even the Confessors, as well as others And the Confessors generally fell off from their Confessions; some saying, they remembred nothing of what they said; others said they had belied themselves and others. Some brake Prison and ran away, and were not strictly searched after, some acquitted, some dismissed, and one way or other all that had been accused were set or left at liberty.

And although had the times been calm, the
condition

condition of the Confeffors might have called
for a *melius inquirendum* ; yet confidering the
combuftion and confufion this matter had
brought us unto; it was thought fafer to under do than over do, efpecially in matters Capital, where what is once compleated cannot
be retrieved : but what is left at one time,
may be corrected at another, upon a review
and clearer difcovery of the ftate of the Cafe.
Thus this matter iffued fomewhat abruptly.

C H A P T E R IV.

HEre was generally acknowledged to be an
error (at leaft on the one hand) but
the Querie is, Wherein ?

A. 1. I have heard it faid, That the Prefidents in *England* were not fo exactly followed,
becaufe in thofe there had been previous quarrels and threatnings of the Afflicted by thofe
that were Condemned for Witchcraft; but
here, fay they, not fo. To which I anfwer.

1. In many of thefe cafes there had been
antecedent perfonal quarrels, and fo occafions
of revenge; for fome of thofe Condemned,
had been fufpected by their Neighbours feveral years, becaufe after quarrelling with their
Neighbours, evils had befallen thofe Neighbours. As may be feen in the Printed Tryals
of *S. M.* and *B. B.* and others : See *Wonders of
the Invifible World, Page* 105. to 137. And
there

there were other like Cases not Printed.

2. Several confessors acknowledged they en-
gaged in the quarrels of other their confederates to afflict persons.   As one *Timothy Swan*
suffered great things by Witchcrafts, as he supposed and testifyed.   And several of the confessors said they did so torment him for the sake
of one of their partners who had some offence
offer'd her by the said *Swan*.   And others
owned they did the like in the behalf of some
of their confederates.

3 There were others that confessed their
fellowship in these works of darkness, was to
destroy the Church of God (as is above in part
rehearsed) which is a greater piece of revenge,
then to be avenged upon one particular person.

2. It may be queried then, *How doth it appear that there was a going too far in this affair?*

A. 1. By the numbers of the persons accused
which at length increased to about an *hundred*,
and it cannot be imagined that in a place of so
much knowledge, so many in so small a com-
pass of Land should so abominably leap into
the Devils lap at once.

2. The quality of several of the accused was
such as did bespeak better things, *and things that
accompany Salvation.* Persons whose blameless
and holy lives before did testify for them.
Persons that had taken great pains to bring up
their *Children in the nurture and admonition of the
Lord :* Such as we had Charity for, as for our
OWN

own Souls: and Charity is a Chriſtian duty commended to us. 1 *Cor.* 13. *Chapt.* *Col.* 3. 14. and in many other Scriptures.

3. The number of the afflicted by Satan dayly increaſed, till about Fifty perſons were thus vexed by the Devil. This gave juſt ground to ſuſpect ſome miſtake, which gave advantage to the accuſer of the Brethren to make a breach upon us.

4. It was conſiderable that Nineteen were Executed, and all denyed the Crime to the Death, and ſome of them were knowing perſons, & had before this been accounted blame-leſs livers. And it is not to be imagined, but that if all had been guilty, ſome would have had ſo much tenderneſs as to ſeek Mercy for their Souls in the way of Confeſſion & ſorrow for ſuch a Sin. And as for the condemned con-feſſors at the Bar, (they being reprieved) we had no experience whether they would ſtand to their Self-condemning confeſſions, when they came to dye.

5. When this proſecution ceaſed, the Lord ſo chained up Satan, that the afflicted grew pre-ſently well. The accuſed are generally quiet, and for five years ſince, we have no ſuch mo-leſtations by them.

6. It ſways much with me that I have ſince heard and read, of the like miſtakes in o-ther places. As in *Suffolk* in *England* about the year 1645. was ſuch a proſecution, until they

ſaw

faw that unlefs they put a ftop it would bring
all into blood and confufion.   The like hath
been in *France*, till 900. were put to Death.
And in fome other places the like ; So that *N.
England* is not the only place circumvented by
the wiles of the wicked and wifely Serpent
in this kind.

Wierus de Praftigiis Demonum, p. 678 Re
lates, *That an Inquifitor in the* Subalpine Valleys,
*enquired after Women Witches, and confumed above
an hundred in the Flames, and daily made new of-
ferings to* Vulcan *of thofe that needed* Helebore
more than Fire. *Until the Country people rofe and
by force of Arms hindred him, and refer the matter
to the Bifhop. Their Husbands men of good Faith
affirmed that in that very time they faid of them,
that they played and danced under a tree, they were
in bed with them.*

R. Burton of Witches &c. p. 158. Saith, *That
in* Chelmstord *in* Eflex, *Anno* 1645 *were Thirty
tryed at once before Judge* Coniers, *and Fourteen
of them hanged, and an hundred more contained in
feveral Prifons in* Suffolk *&* Eflex.

If there were an Error in the proceedings in
other places, and in *N. England*, it muft be in
the principles proceeded upon in profecuting
the fufpected, or in the mifapplication of the
principles made ufe of.   Now as to the cafe at
Salem, I conceive it proceeded from fome miftaken principles made ufe of ; for the evincing
whereof, I fhall inftance fome principles made
ufe

ufe of here, and in other Countrys alfo, which
I find defended by learned Authors writing upon that Subject.

CHAPTER. V.

1. IT hath been believed that Satan cannot
aſſume the Shape of an Innocent perſon,
and in that Shape doe miſchief to the bodies,
or eſtates of mankind.

This *maxim* hath been as the *Primum mobile*,
turning the wheel of accuſation upon perſons
condemned for this Crime in *England* and elſe
where,(ſo far as my reading goeth.) See *Baxter* and *Glanvil*, and other Authors on this Subject. For the inference drawn from hence was,
That when a perſon ſuffers by Diabolical a-
gents and is ſuppoſed to be bewitched, and in
their ſufferings ſee a Spectre in the exact image
of any perſon, that perſon ſo repreſented muſt
be accounted the Witch.

Keeble on the *Common Law*, gives this for a
ground to ſuſpect a perſon for a Witch. Their
Apparition to the ſick party in their fits &c.

In oppoſition to this *Maxim*, I ſhall lay down
three Propoſitions.

1. Satan may and often hath repreſented to
the Imaginations of perſons under bodily
afflictions by him, the ſhape or image of innocent perſons hurting them.

2. Satan can repreſent himſelf to mankind in
a bodily viſible likeneſs.   3.

3. Satans reprefenting himfelf to the fight of men in the fhape of innocent perfons doing mifchief to man, may be without prejudice to, or perverting of Gods Ordinance of Civil Juftice.

1. Satan may reprefent himfelf to the Imaginations &c. I fay *Imagination*; for the Apparition of a perfon to the fick (or obfeffed) perfon in their *fits, may be often times only to their Imaginations. Some of our afflicted perfons have when they come out of their fits declared, that in them they faw an army of men in rank & file; other times the reprefentation of heavenly beauty, white men; and then again fire and hellifh torments. Now all thefe might be only the working of their Phantafies, by Satans prefentations to Imagination, and the like may be of other things and perfons. Yea fome fuch have complained of their own Parents feeming to them to torment them, which might be the abufe of Phantafie.

Yea perfons not under fuch Diabolical impreffions, may by fome difeafe or fores and vapours thence afcending, have the Images of perfons reprefented to their Imagination. Mr. *John Phillips* of *Bofton*, told me, *That he had a fore fwelled Legg, and lying in the warm bed with Eyes open, he faw, as he thought, Women in filk cloathing come to his bed fide, and fpake to them: but a man that ftood by faid there were no Women; whereupon he fufpected the men of Conjuring*

ring tricks ; which moved him to send for a Phy-
sitian three Miles off (for it was nigh Black point.)
and all the time the Messenger was gone, was he
haunted with these Women, as they seemed to him.
The Physitian sent word, that the vapours ascend-
ing from his sore Legg had caused a water in his
Eyes, and disturbance in his Braines, by means
whereof he was troubled with such Visions ; and
sending an eye water to wash his eyes with, and a
cordial to take inwardly ; upon the use of these, this
disturbance vanished in half a quarter of an hour.
If a disease may do this, what may Satan
working upon bodily distempers and vapours
impose upon the Imaginations ?

2. *Prop.* Satan can assume a bodily likeness
and represent himself therein to mans bodily
eyes, that is, if the Lord permit him.

1. He that could make a fire in the Air to
come down upon *Jobs* Sheep, *&c. Job* 1. 16.
Can make a visible Shape and appear, and act
in it as he did in that fire to consume Servants
and Sheep: But so did Satan. Therefore.

2. He that could by *Pharaohs* Sorcerers represent to him Serpents, Froggs & Blood ; and to
Saul dead Samuels Shape ; can assume a bodily
likeness, *&c.* but so did Satan, as *Exod.* 7 & 8.
Chap. 1 *Sam.* 28. of which more hereafter, *&c.*

3. Our Saviour signifies that a Spirit may appear in likeness of a man. *Math.* 14 26, 27. *v.*
compar'd with *Luk.* 24. 36, 37, 38, 39, 40.   Fo.,
(1) The disciples supposed the Person of Christ

to be a Spirit. *Phantasma*, that is a Spectre.
Pneuma, a Spirit *i. e* in bodily likeness, which
shews they had such an apprehension,
that a Spirit could assume a visible bodily likeness. (2.) Christ in answer doth not say, there
can be no such visible representation; but seeks
to satisfy them, by convincing them that it is
himself: *And therefore shews them his hands and
feet. Luk.* 24. thereby to convince them that he
is not a Spirit. (3.) Christ speaks of a Spirit in
general, which comprehends an evil Spirit as
well as a good one.

    4. That Satan appeared to our Saviour when
tempted, *Mat.* 4. 3. at the end of forty days,
in a visible Shape, I prove by these arguments.
    1. It's said Christ was tempted of Satan all
the forty days, *Mar.* 1. 13. and *Luk.* 4. 2. yet
Mat. 4. 2, 3. It's said when he had fasted
fourty days, and was hungry, the Tempter
came to him (*profethion anto*) which implies
another manner of coming to him, and tempting of him, than had been the fourty
days before, and now he spake *Eipen. Mat.* 4.
3, 6, 9. *Legei.* These expressions note Satan
speaking with an audible voice, which implies
a visible bodily shape speaking.
    2. He said *these Stones. Mat.* 4 &c. *Luke* 4.
This *Stone*, as if he had pointed with the finger, or bodily Organ at some peculiar Stone or
Stones, as a corporeal agent.
    3. It is said, Satan taketh Christ up into the
Holy City, setteth him on the Pinacle, taketh

him up into an high Mountain, and sheweth him, brought him to *Jerusalem.* These words Taking, Bringing, Setting. (in Greek, παραλαμβάνει, ίσησι αταγαγ́ον, ήγαγε) are words which are used to note the actings of one bodily agent to another usually.

5. Satan sheweth to the Man Christ, all the *Kingdoms of the World, and the Glory of them, in a moment of time (En stigme Chronou)* in one poynt of time. Now we know the World is round, and that a man can see but a small part of it at once. Therefore that which Satan set before the eyes of Christ, was not all the Kingdoms of the World themselves, but an image and representation of them, and of their Glory, which Satan had framed. And of these might Satan say, as, *Luk.* 4. 6. *All this power will I give thee, and the glory of them: for that is delivered unto me, and to whomsoever I will, I give it.* If then Satan can make an Image of the Kingdoms of the World, and of their glory which is the greater, then can he make the Image of a man, which is the lesser, and appear to a man in such an image : And so appearing can speak and act in and by it as he spake and acted of old by the Serpent unto *Eve,* and by the Possessed in the Gospel. Whether Satan makes such a visible body by gathering the rays called *Species Visibiles,* which flow from every body, whereby its shadow is represented in a Looking-glass and Water, or

as

as the rays of the Sun invisibly scattered in
the Air are by a burning glass contracted and
condensed so as to kindle a Fire, or by other
means, I determine not, But History as well
as the Scripture abundantly testifie, that such
Spirits, or Aieral Bodies have appeared unto
men, called Apparitions or Ghosts. See *Increase Mathers Remarkable Providences*, *Baxter* of
Apparitions, and other Authors. I have also
spoken with very credible persons of discretion and piety that have told me they have
seen such Apparitions when in their perfect
health and senses. But I spare to enlarge.

3. *Proposition* is, Satan may represent himself
doing mischief in the shape of an innocent
person, without prejudice to, or perverting of
Gods Ordinance of Civil Justice.

1. If Satan (can assume the likeness of a
man, as is above proved) then it's alike easy
in it self for him to personate an innocent, as
a guilty person, if we look to his natural power : For according to natural causes by which
he worketh, ones Image is as easly formed as
the others. And no doubt he will sometimes
personate the innocent, unless the Lord restrain him.

2. That Satan hath so done is proved by
Mr. *Increase Mather*, in his *Cases of Conscience*,
Printed *Anno* 1693. by several Histories. To
which I shall add one out of *Wierus de Prestigiis*, *&c. p. 661.*

Among

'Among us (saith he) *A Pretor went to a Conjurer, and by his discovery apprehended many Women, and had them burned (that is for Witches) at last the Conjurer told him, he would shew him one Witch more if he would not take i' amiss,* and impeached the Pretors Wife, and prefixed an hour, when he should see her in a Dance with other Witches. The Pretor consents and calls his friends and kindred to feast with his Wife at that time, and rising from the Table, commands his Wife and Friends to sit still at the Table till he returned. Being carried by the Conjurer where he pleased, he shewed him a Company of Witches in their Dances and unlawful pleasures, and the Pretors Wife with them. Then returning home, he found his friends in the same order he left them, and his Wife with them, and by the testimony of all present, found upon studious enquiry, that his Wife had kept her place in his absence. He opened the matter to them, repenting for punishing the innocent.

3 Satan personating the innocent in doing mischief is no prejudice to Civil Justice, if it can be found out that the mischief so done is the act of Satan, and not the act of the person represented. For what wickedness Satan doth, Satan shall be judged for, and what man doth, man must be judged for. Every one shall bear his own burthen. *Gal* 6 5. And Satans wickedness herein may be found, (most commonly, if not always) by such means as these, if thorough care and diligence be used.

1. If

1. If it can be proved that the party represented was in another place at that time. As
was the case of the *Pretors* Wife above mentioned.

2. If when the afflicted complain they see
John or *Thomas* upon them, pinching, or hurting of them or others, can neither see any person there, nor by feeling perceive any flesh or
bones, they may conclude there's not the very
person complained of, but either an abused I-
magination, or the Devil personating to the
afflicted the person complained of. For Chrifts
rule is, *Luk* 24. 39 *A spirit hath not flesh and
bones as ye see me have.*

3. If the supposed person come into the
room through the Key hole, or when there is
no place open for a person to come in by, then
conclude, its not the person but the Devil seen
there. A Spectre can come in by a pin-hole;
but Satan cannot bring in the body of a man
or woman in at such a place : for if so then Satan could work a miracle properly so called,
which he cannot do. When Chrift came bodily into the midst of the room the doors being shut. *Job* 20. 19, 20. It was a miracle beyond all Satans signs and lying wonders.
The Gospel is confirmed by Gods testimony
with signs and wonders, and divers miracles.
Such Satan cannot do, for then he could subvert our Gospels confimation.

4. When a supposed person is seen in their
full

full proportion and then changed into the form of another Creature, as a Cat, &c. This is a Spectre not the person. The turning Lots Wife into a pillar of Salt was a proper Miracle beyond the power of Devil or Angel of themselves to perform. But a Spectre can change its shape like the Wind under Ice running upon the water. This well weighed will confute many fond Stories that have passed, that such a Woman is a Witch, for she was seen in her full proportion, and then turned into a Cat, and back at last into a Woman; for all this was either a phantasie in the brains, or a Phantasma before the Eyes.

5. If a person (or so esteemed) pass by us on the soft Snow, or dirt, and leave no footsteps behind them, this is to be esteemed a Spectre, and not the real person, unless the person were carried by Satan in the Air. This was brought for an Evidence against a Woman, that she was seen nigh *Malden* in a Moonshiny night passing on the Snow, and left no footsteps behind her; when she might be in her House at *Newbury*, and either the Phantasie of the Witness was abused, or a Spectre passed by him in her Image. Yet if it had been her person so carried by Satan, this would not prove her a Witch, unless her consent were given to it. *Goodwins* Children were carried in the Air by Satan, as saith *Memorable Providences.* P. 14, 15.

D

6. If

6. If the prints of biting of teeth, pinching with fingers, pricking with pins or irons be made on the Bodies of the Afflicted, and no hand, mouth or Body can be seen or felt to do it, this is to be imputed to Satan, and not to a real person doing of it.

By these or such like means, due circumspection being used, when Satan personates the innocent, his fallacy and malice may be discovered, at least ordinarily. Yet if the Lord should suffer Satan so to act, and not be discovered after all means used to find the fallacy (which I never yet read or heard he did) this must be reckoned among the unsearchable acts of Divine Soveraignty, which men may humbly admire ; but not make rules upon such a supposal for humane judicature to proceed upon. These premises considered, we may infer, That if Satan may personate an innocent party to one tormented by him; then, if the Lord permit it, to two, yea to ten. And if once he may do so, then twice, yea, twenty times, if suffered, and yet the person so represented be innocent. And all the danger of injustice being done to that innocent party, ariseth not from Satans acting, so much as from mans mistaken faith and suspicion about Satans act.

Hence then we may confute a vulgar error of people, that will conclude, that such a Woman is, or was a Witch, for she was seen in
the

the Air one night flying Southward, another
time to a Veffel, and other times up into the
Country. When all this time the Devil thro'
Divine permiffion either did it, or impofed upon the Imaginations of the Spectators. And
here we may take notice, that a true faith is fo
pleafing to the Lord, that he doth great things
for his Servants, for their faiths fake ; fo that
Chrift faith, *Mat.* 8. 13 *As thou haft believed,
fo be it done unto thee. All things are poffible to
him that believeth. Great is thy faith, be it unto
thee, as thou wilt. Thy faith hath made thee whole.*
Mark 9. 25. & 10 52. & 15 28. Why may
not a falfe faith in thefe matters provoke the
Lord to fay unto us, *As you believe, be it unto
you?* And let Satan loofe to do ftrange things
as the Accufer of the Brethren, to miflead
them to accufe one another.

CHAPTER VI.

2. **A** Nother Principle much infifted on, is;
That the Devil when he doth harm
to perfons in their Body or Eftate, it is (at
leaft moft commonly, generally and frequently) by the help of our Neighbour : That is,
fome Witch or Conjurer, or fuch like in Covenant with the Devil. Sir *Matthew Hale*, in
his Printed Obfervations upon the Tryal of
thofe Witches he Condemned, (Printed *Anno*
1682.) draws this inference from hence, That
the

the Devil when he hurts the Body or Goods
of men, is in some sort subject to Humane
Justice, though not in himself, yet in his Covenant Servants, by whom he is set a work to
do such mischiefs.

The unsoundness of this principle appeareth
by the Scripture instances of Satans so afflicting man when we read of no Witch to set
him on work. As,

1. When God let Satan loose to try *Jobs*
patience, *Job* 1. *& 2 Chap.*

2. When Satan bound the Body of a Daughter of *Abraham* eighteen years.

3. When Satan tryed the affections of the
Gergesens, and was Gods Instrument to punish
their Worldliness by drowning their Swine,
who ran violently down a steep place (as if
they had been bewitched, according to the o-
pinion of many now a days) into the Sea, being driven of the Devils.

4 We have many Instances of the possessed
with the unclean Spirits that were tormented
and vexed by Satan, to quicken men to prayer,
Mat. 17. 21. and to shew Christs power.

5. Some by their own presumptuous dealing with Satan, have given him power, or at
least opportunity to strip and wound them;
as the *Exorcists, Acts* 19 13. *&c.*

Seeing then we have so many instances of
Satans afflicting without Witches help, and
no clear Scripture instance of his afflicting
                              mankind

mankind in Body, or Estate by Witchcraft;
It's unsafe to conclude generally that those
that are under Diabolical molestations are bewitched. For when persons are perswaded
their Relations are bewitched, they presently
enquire, who is the Witch? and who should
they fasten their suspicions upon, but on these
that the Afflicted cry out against in their fits?

Q. *But is it not evident, that the Afflicted at*
Salem *Village, and parts adjacent,* Anno **1691, 2.**
were Bewitched?

A. Whether those Sufferings by Satan proceeded at first from Witchcraft or no, I shall
leave to a further disquisition.

But as for the most of those Sufferers, I conceive they were such as in the Gospel are called, *Daimonizomenoi. Mat.* 4. 24. *Dæmoniaci*
Dæmoniacks : I do not mean in that degree of
Internal Possession, as those out of whom the
Spirits were cast out. *Mat.* 8. 16. But with
such a degree of external possession or obsession of Satan, which rendred them like the
Demoniacks mentioned, in many things.

1. As they were grievously vexed with the
Devil. (κακως δαιμονιζεται) as the Damsel. *Matt*
15. 22. compare this with *Mark* 7. 25. She
had an unclean Spirit. So were ours vexed
with invisible agents, biting, pricking, pinching
and vexing of them.

I will not say but among so many thus Suffering, some of them at some time might

D 3   counter-

counterfeit part of their Sufferings, and it might be from Satans policy to intangle the whole affair. But for the moſt part they were as thoſe we read of, *Luk. 6. 18. Vexed with unclean Spirits.*

2. We read, *Mat. 17. 15.* of them that *oft-times fell into the fire and into the water, being Lunatick*; but were caſt this way & that by an Evil Spirit. *Mark 9. 17, to 30.* So were ſome of ours by an evil ſpirit tranſported from place to place, and in danger of being burnt, or drowned, but that Satan was reſtrained, as in caſe above ſaid.

3. The poſſeſſed man, *Mark. 5. 4.* had more than humane ſtrength in breaking fetters and chains. So ſome of theſe in their fits performed that which was above their owr ſtrength.

4. The poſſeſſed damſel, *Act. 16. 16* did by the Devil ſoothſay ; that is, diſcover ſecrets in a prophetical way : (ſhe did *manteuein.*) So ſome of theſe did by the Devils means tell of perſons and things, abſent and future, as when ſuch another fit ſhould come again, *&c.* where ſuch a perſon abſent was, and what he did : inſomuch that had they been *Sui juris,* perſons free from Diabolical obſeſſion, and overpowering force, they might juſtly have been queſtioned for dealing with a familiar Spirit. But the force they were under was their vindication, as it was here, *Act. 16. 16.*

5. The

5. The possessed of old were some of them exceeding fierce. *Mat.* 8. 28. So were some of these afflicted persons fierce, troublesome and mischievous in their fits, beyond their natural temper and behaviours at other times. From these things compared together, why may we not judge these demoniacks, as well as those in the Gospel? And that its possible for Satan in these times to afflict thus without Witches, as well as in those? Seeing these did also in their fits *some, gnash their teeth and pine away,* as he did, *Mark* 9 18.

And here we may observe the weakness of the signs given by the *Common Law,* to know who is bewitched; (which signs as *Keeble* faith, are taken out of the tryals in *Lancashire,* and from *Bernard*:)

For the first sign given is; The wasting of a person and the cause unknown : This sign is very fallible : for,

1. The wasting may proceed from an unknown disease. And the ignorance of Physitians may ascribe that to Witchcraft which proceeds from a natural hidden disease.

2. *Jobs* sore boyles from head to foot came from Satan without Witchcraft, and the cause of them was most probably hidden from the common practice of Physitians.

The second sign they give is, When two persons are taken together in the like strange fits. This may be a sign of persons possessed, and

hapned

hapned often in the experiences at *Salem*, among the persons possessed, as abovesaid.

The third sign given is, When the afflicted party truly telleth what the suspected person is doing at a distance. This is rather a sign of a person possessed.

And we find the two men possessed, *Matth.* 8. 28. &c. had like fits, for both kept among the Tombs, both were exceeding fierce, so as to hinder persons passing that way, both together made the same outcry to Jesus, that he should not torment them. These things shew a unity among the Devils afflicting them: but no unity of Witches joyning with them.

Fourth sign is, When the afflicted out of their fits knew nothing what they did, or said in them. But this (if our obsessed or possessed persons said truly) often fell out in the tormented at *Salem.*

Fifth sign, Supernatural strength in their fits. Now this is a sign of the possessed, *Mark* 5. 4. Who in their fits brake chaines and fetters.

Sixth sign is, When the afflicted vomit pins, nailes, irons, &c. To this I say, whether these pins, nailes, &c are by the Devil brought invisibly to the mouths of the persons so vomiting and so cast out from their mouths, but not out of their stomacks or throats ; or whether they are insensibly conveyed by the working of Satan into the stomacks or throats of the persons vomiting, and so vomited forth, neither the one

nor

nor the other, can certainly prove the vomiter
bewitched, unless it be made manifest that Satan doth thus vex the party by confederacy
with a Witch.   But where Satan hath a permission to vex and possess a person he may do
these things, as well as other things he did unto
the possessed mentioned in the Gospels.

The seventh sign is, The afflicted person
having the sight of the apparition of the suspected party, and when the mischief of a fit or
the like following shortly after.   Now it having been already proved, that Satan can represent, to those that are possessed, innocent persons : it is not to be wondered that Satan
should represent to the eyes or imagination of
a possessed sufferer, a Spectre representing a
suspected innocent person just before he casteth
them into a fit, especially seeing hereby he
gaines upon the credulity of the possessed, and
their friends, for the accusing an innocent, and
it may be a godly person ; for this helps forward his design as the accuser of the brethren.
Rev. 12. 10.

I would then from these considerations infer,
That if a party handled as in the seven particulars above expressed, cannot thereby be said
to be bewitched, Then there is no need, unless
somewhat else appear, to trouble our selves to
enquire who is the Witch that troubleth such
a party.

CHAP.

CHAPTER. VII.

3. ANother principle Improved in these Enquiries is, When the party suspected looks upon the parties supposed to be bewitched, and they are thereupon struck down into a fit, as if struck with a Cudgel. This bewitching by the eye is an opinion Seventeen Hundred years old,

Nescio quis teneros oculis mibi fascinat agnos. Virgil.

Mr. *Gaul* in his Book, Printed 1648. page 128. Saith, *Some Witches by inspecting, or looking on, but to a glance, or squint, or peep at with an envious eye, is sufficient to effascinate.* And we may find much use made of this experiment in Tryals in *England* mentioned by *Baxter, Glanvil* and *Burton.* And however this seemed a presumption at *Salem Village*, yet at length it was apparent to be a delusion of Satan. For this experiment was found at the Tryals of persons when the Accused sought to clear themselves, and it cannot be conceived that then they would act Witchcraft to hasten their own Condemnation : And no person can be said to act Witchcraft against their own will and consent.

Again, we read, *Mark* 9. 20. That when the possessed was brought unto Christ, and saw Christ, then the Spirit tare him, and he fell to the ground and wallowed foaming. So that

that the Devil chose this time and place to
cast the possessed into a fit even in the presence
of Christ.   Let us then consider these Afflicted to be Demoniacks, and we must own, it's
in Satans power to cast them into a fit in the
presence, and upon the sight of the Accused.
And if this may increase the suspicion against
the Accused, it's for his interest to chuse such
a time.

4. Another presumption made use of hath
been to cause the suspected to touch the party
supposed to be bewitched, and if that touch
bring the party out of their fit, this hath been
esteemed by many a strong suspicion at least,
as may be read in some of the fore cited Authors.

And Mr. *Glanvil* supposeth a Philosophical
reason for it, *viz*. that the Witch by the cast
of her eye sends forth a Malefick Venome
into the Bewitched to cast him into a fit, and
therefore the touch of the hand doth by a
sympathy cause that venome to return into
the Body of the Witch again. As when a
person is stung by a Snake, the application of
the Body or flesh of the same Snake to the
wound will draw back the poyson into its
former fountain. But the truth is both these
effects depend upon the Devils free agency :
And he frames his things much according to
the opinion of the Spectators, with intent to
deceive.   I never could see reason to justify

fy such a kind of Tryal (though allowed by
Bernard as lawful to be used ;) but since I
have more considered it, I look upon it very
unwarrantable to be used, being as it were the
putting a staff into the hand of Satan, to try
what he will do with it. For the recovery of
the party out of the Fit hereby must be from
a natural or divine cause, or from the Devil:
We cannot prove either of the two former,
and if the third, its but the Devils testimony,
and therefore not to be used by us.

5. Another practice hath been when the
party suspected is in Prison, and the Afflicted
cry out they are miserably tormented by
them: If then the suspected party be bound,
and the afflicted person thereupon, have ease
or release of their fits, then this is a presumption
that the suspected party is guilty. This was
used at *Isanbal, Anno* 1661. (see *Glanvil, page*
168.) and the success answered the expectation.

But this is no ground so much as of suspicion, because it depends either upon some physical efficacy in binding to give the party ease,
or upon the precontract of the suspected made
with Satan, or from the voluntary act of the
Devil ceasing to afflict at such a time ; neither
of the two former can be proved: not any
physical vertue in the binding the party; for
how can cords bind a Spirit, and as for the

Contract

Contract with Satan, that remains yet to be proved, and if such there be, yet the terms of it are to us unknown ; and the Devil being a Lyar from the beginning, will keep or break his own promises, fo as fuites the intereft of his Kingdom. So that in fuch cafes we can afcribe the releafe of the afflicted only to Satans agency and policy by fuch a vile abufing the mifchief of thofe which make the tryal.

6 The like is to be faid when a Demoniack finds eafe of their fits upon the apprehending, or condemning, or Execution of the perfon complained againft. For that eafe may come by Satans policy, defifting his rage to confirm our error : or from Divine Favour in anfwer of prayer, or pity to the diftreffed.

C H A P T E R.   VIII

7.   A Seventh principle is, If the party fufpected appear in Spectre to the afflicted, and the afflicted give a blow with a knife, fword, &c. unto the Spectre (or fome other in their behalf) and the Spectre feems wounded, or bleeding, or to have their garment torn, or flit by the blow received. And that the party Spectrally reprefented be prefently fearched, and there is found upon their body a wound, or blood, &c. on the fame part of their body, or a rent, or cut upon the fame part of

the

the garment, which appeared upon the Spectre unto the afflicted. This hath been counted a strong evidence to prove the party suspected to be a confederate with Satan in afflicting the complainer. As by Judge *Archer* in *Coxes* case, Executed at *Taunton*, *Anno* 1663. (See *Glanvil part 2. p.* 196.) But let us search this to the bottom ; and there is no ground of suspicion in such a kind of probation. For the ground of the suspicion ariseth hence. *viz.* That what wound or mark is given to the Spectre (that is to the Devils aerial assumed body) is transla- ted thence unto the person setting this Spectre on work to afflict ; or to their garments, if the mark be on that. But we have no sufficient ground to know this.

1. For if it must be so, it must be either (1.) From some sympathy in nature between the Spectre and the party represented by it. But this we have no ground in reason to conclude ; for whence or how should such a sympathy be between an humane body, and the Devil in the Image or likeness of it ? Or if it were, how can there come such a sympathy between the garment of a person and the Devil appearing in the likeness of that garment ? Surely the garment was not in any league with Satan ? (2.) Or this comes to pass by vertue of the Co- venant between Satan and this confederate : if so we say, I ask how come we to know there is such an article in the bargain with the De- vil ?

vil ? or if we know there were such an article
in their agreement, how can we tell, that the
Devil will stand to his own Covenant ? Or,
(3.)This comes to pass by the Immediate hand
of God making such a translation of a wound
&c. unto a Witch that they may thereby be
discovered ; which if so, it is preternatural if
not supernatural. And we have no ground
from Scripture to expect such a sign from God ;
and therefore to expect it is to be guilty of the
sin of that Wicked Generation, that sought after
a sign. *Math.* 16. 4. *Which should not be given
to them.*   Or (.4) This translation cometh (if
there be any such) from the Devil as a free &
powerful Spirit, afflicting the body or affecting
the garment so marked : And if it be from
hence, its the Devils testimony which ought to
be no credit with mankind.

2. The true state of this case seems to be
this ; That the person or garment so represented to the Afflicted by a Spectre was wounded, or bleeding, or cut or rent before.   And
the Devil knowing this, represents to the afflicted
(or striker at the Spectre) that part of the Spectre
which answers the Body wounded, or garment
rent or torn, the Searchers finding such wounds
upon, or rents about the person suspected are
ready to conclude it was done by the stroke at
the Spectre which was done before.   I shall
confirm this by instances.

There was at *Chelmsford,* an Afflicted person,

fon, that in her fits cryed out againſt a Woman, a Neighbour, which Mr. *Clark,* the Mi-
niſter of the Goſpel there could not believe
guilty of ſuch a Crime.   And it hapned while
that woman was milking her Cow, the Cow ſtruck
her with one horn upon her Forehead and
fetched blood, and while ſhe was bleeding, a
Spectre in her likeneſs appeared to the party
Afflicted, who pointing at the Spectre, one
ſtruck at the place, and the Afflicted ſaid, you
have made her forehead bleed. Hereupon
ſome went to the woman, and found her forehead bloody, and acquainted Mr. *Clark* with
it; who forthwith went to the woman, and
asked how her forehead became bloody, and
ſhe anſwered by a blow of the Cows horn, as
above ſaid; whereby he was ſatisfied that it
was a deſign of Satan to render an innocent
perſon ſuſpected.

Another inſtance was at *Cambridge,* about
fourty years ſince. There was a man much
troubled in the night with Cats, or the Devil in
their likeneſs haunting of him, whereupon he
kept a light burning, and a Sword by him as
he lay in bed; for he ſuſpected a Widow
woman to ſend theſe Cats or Imps by Witchcraft to bewitch him. And one night as he
lay in bed, a Cat or Imp came within his
reach, and he ſtruck her on the back; and
upon enquiry heard this Widow had a ſore
back; this confirmed his ſuſpicion of the Widow,

dow, he, suppofing that it came from the
wound he gave the Cat. But Mr. *Day* the
Widows Chyrurgeon cleared the matter ; faying, this Widow came to him and complained
of a fore in her back, and becaufe fhe could
not fee it, defired his help ; and he found it to
be a Boyl, and ripened and healed it as he
ufed to do other Boyls. But while this was
in cure, the fuppofed Cat was wounded as already rehearfed.

But fome may fay when fuch wounds or
rents come, it's not the Spectre that's ftruck
but the real perfon or garment is there prefent,
but by vertue of the Charm, or Witchcraft, a
mift is caft between the Witch and Spectators
in the room, whereby the perfon becomes invifible to all of them, except the bewitched
Sufferer. As fome juglers have feemed to creep
through a Tree or Log, when indeed its only
upon the Tree or Log ; but by inchantment a
fhadow of the Log or Cloud is caft over the
Log between the Jugler and Spectators, whereby they are deceived.

I Anfwer, If it were fo, then thofe that
ftrike with Sword, or other Inftrument, and
wound the party might feel fome body, or
garment ftopping the force of their blow ; for
a Body can be felt if it cannot be feen, as a-
bove fhewed. But when the ftricken inftrument feels no harder fubftance than Air to ftop
its force, and there feems to be motion in the

E   way

way to the Afflicted's eye : We may conclude
its but a Spectre, or deluded imagination.

CHAPTER IX.

8. IF after Cursing there follows Death, or
at least some mischief: This saith *Perkins* (in his Discourse of Witchcraft, *Chap.* 7,
Sect. 2.) This is a presumption. For Witches
are wont to practise their mischievous facts by
cursing and banning. This also is a sufficient
matter of Examination.

I acknowledge when persons curse or threaten others to kill them, or do other mischief to
their Bodies or Estates, and the mischief threatned is performed as threatned ; here is ground
so far to suspect the threatner, as to question
them about it, unless it appeareth to be performed by some other person or cause. So if
after Cursing there follows Death, *&c.* And
it appeareth to be done by Witchcraft, this is
a ground to suspect and examine the threatner, unless there be grounds to suspect some
other Author of the Witchcraft. But as the
proposition is laid down generally by Mr. *Perkins*, as a general rule I conceive it's unsafe.

1 Because such death, or mischief oftimes
proceed from other causes, so that there is no
ground to impute them to Witchcraft. For,

1. Some persons are of such hasty spirits and
untruly

unruly tongues, that their mouth is dayly full of curfing and bitternefs, *Rom.* 3. 14.

2. There be few Houſe-keepers, where are many in Family and a Stock about them ; but that by the hand of God, Death at ſome times enters upon ſome perſon in the Family, and Cattel ſometimes dye by Diſeaſes and Caſualties : Who is there that hath an Eſtate, but at ſome times they meet with loſſes ?

3. Hence it falls out that theſe calamities, ſome of them happen at or nigh ſome one time of their angry neighbours curſing, who had curſed them ten times before, or threatned them, and yet no ſuch calamity enſued. And this their laſt threatning had no more influence upon the evil befalling the Family, than the ten cauſeleſs Curſes that went before, as *Prov.* 26. 2. What then doth all this prove ? A tongue ſet on fire, and it may be from hell ; but not a Covenant with Hell to procure the calamities that befal their Neighbours.

Again, ſome are of ſuch a ſuſpicious temper, that they are apt to impute all ſad accidents that do befal them, to proceed from Witchcraft, and thereby in ſuffering times are apt to be jealous of their Neighbours that come frequently to their Houſes in their day of adverſity, as cauſers of theſe afflictions by ſome charming or inchantment.

Again, It may be Queried, Whether Satan may not ſometimes take advantage upon the

times

times when neighbours contend with, and
threaten thofe that live by them, to do fome
hurt to the Bodies or Goods of thofe threatned, that thereby he may caft upon the party
threatned, the impu ation of Sorcery. Doubt-
lefs as he is *the Accufer of the Brethren, Rev.* 12
He would fo do if the Lord will permit him
to indanger the life of the threatner. And
who can tell but that the Lord may permit
him at fometimes fo to do, for a juft punifhment to fuch unbridled tongues ? I remember, that above fourty years ago, when there
was a great difcourfe about Witches ; *A very
holy man heard his Wife fay, fhe defired a fucking
Pig ; and he going to a Neighbour's houfe, faw a
Sow with a litter of Pigs, and took a phantafie to
one of them in particular for his Wife, and asked
the Owner for that Pig ; the Owner denied him:
Hereupon he went away in a great paffion, very
unfuitable to fuch a perfon. And that very Pig
left its dam and Company, and followed this man
to his home.* This was obferved in the day of
it, it was fuppofed Satan might have fome
hand in it, taking advantage upon the paffion
of fo good a man, to render him fufpeded by
fuch an accident if he could.

9. If any perfon, man or woman be noto-
rioufly defamed for fuch a party. This *Perkins (eodem loco)* makes a prefumption. But
in truth there is no weight in this, unlefs thofe
neighbours among whom the fufpeded party
                                        lived

lived had good grounds for their suspicion:
Because many persons have drunk in false
principles about the tokens by which a Witch
is to be known ; and judge of persons accord-
ding to those false principles (some of which
are above recited) which may asperse the
most innocent and righteous person living.
Our Saviour was slandered as if he *cast out De-*
vils by Belzebub the Prince of Devils, Mat. 12:
24. And the Disciple is not above his Master,
Mat. 10. 25. Some persons will put an evil
construction upon an innocent action, and so
raise an evil fame against a person ; and then
others believing it, are apt to look upon other
actions with a squint eye, and through the
multiplying glass of their own jealousies, make
a Mole-hill seem a Mountain, to render an
hated or despised neighbour evil spoken of.

10. If the party suspected be the Son or
Daughter, or Man-servant, or Maid servant,
or familiar friend, near Neighbour, or old
Companion of a known and convicted Witch.
This may be a presumption, saith *Perkins.* But
unto all these it may be said, there is no more
ground to suspect any person of this crime
upon such relations or circumstances, then
there is to presume a person is a Thief, or
Murderer, or Drunkard, *&c.* because he is the
Child, Servant, Neighbour, *&c.* of a Thief,
Murderer, Drunkard, or the like, convicted

Crimi-

Criminal. Which may be, or may not be if the Lord incline the heart of him or her that is so related, to abhor such wickedness. As the Wheat and Tares grow together in the same Field : So Good and Wicked in the same Neighbourhood, Family ; yea, and lying in the same Bed, *so that one shall be taken, and the other left, Mat.* 24. 40, 41. *Luk.* 17. 34, 35, 36. The Lord saith, *The Son shall not dye for the sin of the Father, Ezek.* 18. 14 *&* 21. *ver.* If the Son, (Servant or Neighbour, or Companion) seeth the sins of his Father, *&c.* and doth not the like, *&c.* he shall not dye, *&c.* which shews that these so related may and sometimes do see and abhor the ways of wickedness, those so near unto them walk in, and abhor them, therefore they are not to be suspected, meerly upon that account.

11. Some make this a presumption. If a person sick and dying, doth take it upon his or her Death, that such an one hath bewitched them. See *Perkins Chap.* 7. *page* 210. So *Keeble* on the Common Law, saith, the testimony of the person hurt upon their death complaining against a person, that they appeared to them and bewitched them. Now in this case it must be considered whether this dying person were not under Diabolical Molestations, or an abused phantasie, or under ungrounded suspicions of the party they complained of before they were so sick. And the grounds of
their

their fufpicions are to be thorowly confidered, before the furvivers make this a ground of fuf-picion. Sure all this may proceed from falfe principles (as there Expreffed) drunk in by a well meaning, but miftaken dying perfon.

CHAPTER X.

12. SOme faith *Perkins*, do add this for a pre-fumption. If the party fufpected be found to have the Devils mark: for it is com-monly thought, when the Devil maketh his Covenant with them, he always leaveth his mark behind him. *Bernard* makes it a ground of Conviction. (*Gaul* only a prefumption.) And *Tertullian* (who lived above 1400 years ago) fays, It's the Devils cuftom to mark his; and note, faith *Bernard*, That this mark is in-fenfible, and being pricked, it will not bleed, fometimes like a teat (and the Devil fucks, or toucheth them:) fometimes but a blewifh fpot, fometimes a red one, and fometimes the flefh funk.

I conceive fuch a mark is neither ground of conviction or fufpicion.

1. Becaufe the Lord fometimes in anger, and fometimes for tryal of his Servants, fends fuch marks upon the Bodies of men, as are un-ufual; as the *Emerods upon the Philiftins*, I *Sam.* 5, 6, 7. Which made thofe Heathens fay, *The Hand of the God of Ifrael is fore upon us.* And

E 4 *Deut.*

Deut. 28. 27, 35. *God threatens to punish his peo-*
ple for their sins, with a botch, emerods and with
the Itch whereof they could not be healed. So then
some of these sores might constantly be moist
as if they had been sucked.

2. Many persons have naturally, or by some
sickness or hurt, received some sores, like, if not
the same with those they call the Devils marks.
I knew a man, that lived and dyed without the
least suspicion of that crime, that told me he
had a natural issue upon his breast from his
youth up, which distilled about a drop or two
in twenty four hours, so that it was alwayes
moist, and conduced much to his health. And
as for the weaker Sex ; The Lord hath said
unto *Eve,* and her Daughters, *In sorrow shall be*
thy Conception; but instanceth not in the particulars. But experience hath shewed upon some
sober and pious women, after hard Travels and
the like, that they have had those Excrescences which are called, *Pili Uteri.* And I have
been informed by a skilful Midwife that hath
known vertuous women that have had those
Piles, and that they are without sence of feeling, sometimes and after cold, handling, *&c.*
are apt to draw up into the Body. Satan
knows who hath (by the hand of God) such
suspected marks, which the Lord lays on them
as their affliction, & if he can by other means
get them to be suspected, and their Bodies
searched, he will hereby expose them to great-

er

er suspicion, it not Condemnation ; if we take
this for a ground of conviction or presumption
of guilt.   But if he attains not that, yet hereby
shall sober and innocent persons be exposed to
the reproach of such, who when they understand God hath loosed their cord, and afflicted
them, will as *Job* speaks, *marr their path, set
forward their calamity, and not spare to spit in
their face.* *Job* 30. 10, 11, 12, 13. For he or
she that is ready to slip with his or her foot, is
as a lamp despised in the thought of him that is
at ease.   And there may be such Excrescences
from a natural cause, which yet Learned Physitians cannot find out, the reason of.   Man
knows but in part the Works of God, *Eccles.* 11.
5. *For he doth great things, and unsearchable ;
marvellous things without number.*

3. If we enquire how these are known to
be the marks of one in league with Satan? It
must come from the Confession of Witches,
that have owned such things.

Now among the many Confessors at *Salem*,
there were sundry declared they had such
marks on them: one in her head which she
said the Devil in likeness of a bird came daily,
and pecked, or sucked.   I saw the sore place
and there was nothing to be seen to make it to
differ from another sore coming by natural
causes.   Another said, she had the Devils mark
upon her leg, which was a blew spot as broad
as a Shilling : her Husband testifyed, that he
saw the spot, but little suspected it to be the De-

vils mark. Others had fores on other parts of
their bodies which they faid the Devil fucked;
but by all that, I could learn by thofe that faw
them, there was nothing to demonftrate that
they came in a preternatural way by Satan;
but only the parties own affirmation: which
whether true or falfe I leave to God and time
farther to difcover. And I fuppofe we had as
many confeffions and demonftrations to render
what they faid credible, as hath been known at
any one time in fome Ages. But be it fo, that
by the confeffions of known Witches there
have been upon fome of the bafer fort (as *Bernard* faith) of them, fuch teats, or marks.
Thefe may come by natural caufes, or violent
cafualties, and by Satan be perverted to fuch an
ufe. But if they come from Satan immediately as the confeffors acknowledge. This can
only tend to the conviction of thofe that fo
confefs, and where thofe marks are found:
but make nothing to the proof, or fufpicion of
other perfons to be guilty of that crime, who
having fuch marks deny the crime, and afcribe
thefe bodily marks to other caufes. So that its
far more fafe wholly to lay afide the practice
of fearching after fufpected perfons teats or
Witch marks, unlefs in thofe who confefs themfelves to have them, and that for tryal to fee
whether they fay true, or not; then by ufing
it to lay ftrefs upon a fallible fign.

13. Another

13 Another unsafe principle is to lay weight upon the testimony of Ghosts, as they are called ; that is to say, *Spectres* appearing in the shape of the dead, and personating them. Satan by his wiles in this kind hath gained too much credit, in hours of Temptation. For it hath so happened, that when in the death of some persons there was any notice of a circumstance which might give unto a jealous eye, any colour for suspicion, that any one was accessary to their death ; the Spectre personating them hath cryed out to the afflicted for vengeance against such an one for murdering them, telling the manner how, by relating the circumstances of their death : and presently people were ready to say, I remember those very circumstances in the dying of such a person. Well, it is very probable such an one murdered the party. And hereby the person suspected is accused of Witchcraft and Murder together, and by joyning these accusations together, both seem the more probable and credible. But that there is no reason to hearken to such accusations will appear if we consider.

1. That Satan can assume the shape of living innocents, as above shewed, and therefore of the dead also ; as of dead *Samuel* : and that shape being assumed can say what he pleaseth, or seem to the Imagination of *daimoniacal* persons so to speak. And he being *a Lyar from the beginning, Joh. 8. 44.* By his lyes he fastens what

accu-

accusation he pleaseth of murder, or other crime upon the living. And if hearkened unto will, as the deceived *Eve*, by falsely accusing God, deceive us by falsely accusing our Neighbour to us.

I know Hystories speak of Ghosts discovering murders, at sometimes, and moneys lost, or acts of injustice done in the life time of the person represented by the said Ghost; which some have conceived to be the very Soul of the deceased : (and by this opinion many *Papists* have been confirmed in the error of *Purgatory*:) Some a good Angel sent in that Similitude to procure justice to be done: and some have conceived it to be the Devil compelled, *Volens Nolens*, to discover injustice, *or transforming himself into an Angel of Light*, as 2 *Cor.* 11. 14 by seeming zealous for justice. I should digress too far from my intended scope to discuss, what may be said *pro* or *con* in this matter. It sufficeth in the case, *Anno* 1692. To say we have had so much experience of the wiles of Satan appearing in the likeness of the living, that we have no reason to believe him in the likeness of the dead.

2. The hearkening after Ghosts, if we take not heed, may hurry us unawares into that sin forbidden, *Isai.* 8. 19 *Viz. Seeking for the living to the dead:* What? shall we hearken to or enquire of the dead, what they can say against the living? This hath a tendency to that iniquity

quity forbidden, *Deut*. 18. 11. by the name of *Necromancy* : in Hebrew it is, *Vedoresh-el Hammetbim*. A seeker unto the dead.

A like unto this deceit of Satan, was another of his devices. *Viz*. He would appear Spectrally in the shape of a Neighbour unto the afflicted, and say, I killed such and such a person, and relate in that shape the manner of the deceased's departure out of the world, by plausible and seemingly true circumstances which was in the day of it, too much credited to augment Suspicions against the accused : But the invalidity of such accusations appears by what is already spoken concerning the Apparition of Ghosts.

CHAPTER. XI.

14. SOme have laid great weight upon this, When something supposed to be bewitched, or to contain the charm by which the inchantment is wrought is burned in the fire, and the party suspected comes to the fire, or seems to be burnt after it, or by such like ways concerned ; this hath been esteemed a farther presumption that they are guilty. As in Sir *Mathew Hale* his condemning *Amy Duny*, Printed *Anno* 1682. A toad found in the blanket of *Durent* (said to be bewitched) was held in the fire till it made an horrible noise, and the next day *Amy Duny* (who was suspected to bewitch *Durent*) was found all grievously scorch-
ed

ed with the fire. The use of such experiments is justly condemned by *Perkins* and others, as after a sort a practice of Witchcraft : Yet the seeming discovery hereby made hath found entertainment by those that oppose the means used.

But before we give credence to such a discovery, we must be very circumspect least we be deceived by humane knavery ; as happened in a case nigh *Richmond* Island, *circiter Anno* 1659.

One *Mr.* Thorpe *a drunken Preacher, was gotten in to Preach at* Black point *under the appearance and profession of a Minister of the Gospel, and boarded at the house of Goodman* Bayly*, and* Bay*lyes Wife observed his Conversation to be contrary to his calling, gravely told him his way was contrary to the Gospel of Christ, and desired him to reform his Life or leave her house. So he departed from the house, and turned her Enemy, and found an opportunity to do her an injury : and it so fell out that Mr.* Jordan *of* Spurwink *had a Cow dyed and about that time Goody* Bayly *had said, she intended such a day to travel to* Casco-Bay*. Mr.* Thorpe *goes to Mr.* Jordans *man or men and saith, the Cow was bewitched to death, and if they would lay the carcass in a place he should appoint, he would burn it, and bring the Witch : and accordingly the Cow is laid by the path that led from* Black point *to* Casco *and set on fire that day Goody* Bayly *was to travel that way, and so she came by while the Carcass was in burning, and* Thorpe *had her questioned*
for

for a Witch: But Mr. Jordan interposed in her behalf: and said his Cow dyed by his Servants negligence, and to cover their own fault they were willing to have it imputed to Witchcraft; and Mr. Thorpe *knew of* Goody Baylyes *intended Journey, and orders my Servants (said he) without my approbation, to burn my Cow in the way where* Bayly *is to come; and so unriddled the knavery, and delivered the innocent.*

But suppose the case where there is no such deceit, and the suspected party comes to it, when such a thing is burned, or seems extraordinarily hurt or concerned at such a time, how will this prove the party guilty of the crime, he or she is suspected of? If any way, it must (1.) Proceed from some natural cause, or sympathy in nature, between the thing burned, and the Witches Body; but no reason can be given of this; for a charm is wrought by the Devils power, and not by any natural power of the Sorcerer, conveying any natural venome from their own body, which by the operation of the fire should revert back into it again, as to its center or fountain. (2) Or from the immediate hand of God, causing this effect for discovery of the Guilty; which we have no warrant from the Word of God to expect (as was said in another case, *Chapt.* 8.) (3) Or by means of the person burning the thing, & using it as a charm to find out the person that laid the inchantment upon the thing burnt;
which

which if it be affirmed truly, would rather
prove the burner the Sorcerer ; and so tend
to clear the suspected. (4.) Or it proceeds
from the Compact made between the Devil
and the Sorcerer ; which if any affirm, I ask
how know you there is any such Covenant
made ? that is first to be proved, and then that
this is one article in that Covenant, and that
the Devil will attend to, and keep his part of
the Covenant inviolable. Neither of which
can be demonstrated. (5.) Or this suffering is
a meer phantasie, or the free agency of the
Devil, who is a lyar from the beginning, and
therefore not to be heeded. This Experiment
is like the ways of trying by water, fire, bot-
tling of Urine, &c. all which have been justly
condemned as a sort of charms to be rejected
by Christians.

Among the Confessors, *Anno* 1692. was a
Negro Woman, who charged two women to
make her a Witch, describing how she see her
mark in the Devils Book. And said, if she
might be permitted, she would fetch the things
whereby she tormented the afflicted complainers. And accordingly brought an Handker-
chief, wherein several knots were tyed, raggs of
Cloth, a piece of Cheese and a piece of grass.
And as I was credibly informed, some compelled her to swallow the grass, & that night she was
burned in her flesh ; and one took a piece of
her ragg and burnt it in the fire, and one of
the

the Afflicted that had complained of her, was presently burned on the hand. Another piece of her rags was put under water, and then others complainants were choaked, and strived for breath as if under water: And another ran to the River as if she would drown her self. Here note, that the raggs on which, as the Confessor said, the Witchcraft was laid, did when put into fire and water, affect the persons supposed to be thereby bewitched more than the Charmer her self. And probably the cause may be, that Satan, the Lord permitting him, may inflict his mischief on the person, the Spectators or Actors herein suppose to be concerned, suiting hereby his design to mans faith about it. And if so, the reason why any suspected person is hereby concerned, is not because they are guilty, but because they are suspected.

15. If the above named Signs singly taken, are not sufficient to prove a person guilty of this Crime; then when many, or most of these suspicions above named center upon the same person, they cannot prove them guilty. Nay, all of them may be fixed upon the same person, by the wiles of the Devil, and yet the person be innocent. For if Satan can assume & afflict any one in the shape of an innocent, as hath been already proved, he may also in shape of a Ghost of the deceased accuse them, and so

F a3

act over and suspicions mentioned.

Quæ singula non prosunt junct a non juvant.

I find in the tryals and condemnations that
have been in *England* & *Ireland*, several of them
have proceeded upon sundry of these suspicions
put together; and so the total thence arising
hath amounted to a condemnation. See *Glanvil, part.* 2. *pag.* 118. to 209. In particular in
the case of *Julian Cox* before Judge *Arsher, An.*
1663. *pag.* 194.

But probably it may be said, that the methods
which I except against have been used with
good success, for by such things Witchcrafts &
Witches have been discovered, & some brought
to confession and repentance, and given unde-
niable demonstrations of the reality of their
guilt, and recovery after it out of that snare of
the Devil, and therefore such ways of discovery
are still to be used.

Ans. 1. Let us take it for granted, that
these means have occasioned the discovery of
Witches; yet if any of them are unlawful they
are not to be used because of former success.
Many things have been done irregularly which
God hath turned to a good event; as the lying of *Jacob* to get the birthright; the selling
of *Joseph* by his Brethren. Yea, the diabolical
divination of *Nebucadnezar. Ezek.* 21. 21. to 25.
vers. proved prosperous to him. And *Balaams*
inchantments to procure a curse, God turned
into a blessing to *Israel*. Yet none of these
things

things are to be imitated by us upon hope of the like event to follow.

2. If the discovery abovesaid hath followed upon the use and dependance upon the means abovesaid, it may be said to come from Satan (over-ruled by the Lord to subserve his glorious purposes) as the instrument of discovery, who exposeth at some times his own Vassals to humane justice, that he may cut them off from the earth: and therefore assumes their shapes or otherwise renders them suspected to their Neighbours upon such kind of presumptions, as may wrap in the guilty and innocent together, and thereby working upon the erroneous principles of men, doth (as we use to say, kill two birds with one stone,) deliver up his own Servant to ruine, and give occasion for the condemnation thereby of an innocent person. But Satan is not to be trusted when he speaks truth, or doth that which eventually proveth good, because his aim is always to do mischief thereby. Our Saviour Christ would not accept Satans worship and testimony when he spake true. *Mark* 5. 6, 7. 8. And *Paul* was grieved in spirit when the Devil gave an high testimony of him to be the Servant of the most high God. *Act*. 16. 16, 17, 18.

CHAP.

CHAPTER. XII.

16. B*Ernard* faith, Witches may be convicted
by their *Extasies* : with the delight
whereof, Witches are so taken, that they will
hardly conceal the fame : or however at some
time or other they may be found in them.
But the infufficiency of this kind of proof will
appear by confidering the various forts of *Extafies*, and the diverfe fubjects of them. *Extafies*
are either natural, divine or diabolical.

1. *Natural*, which proceeds from the confti-
tution of the body, and fome violent difeafe, as,
Feaver, &c. whereby the imagination is ftrang-
ly tranfported, and the party conceiveth himfelf to be in fome glorious place & company &c.
which proves but a meer dream of a man eating
and drinking, but when he awaketh his foul is
empty. *Ifa* 29 8.

2. *Divine*, as the trances of *Peter*, *Act*. 10.10,
and of *Paul*, *Act* 22 17

3 Or *Diabolical*, of *Witches*, perfons *Obfeffed*,
or *Poffiffed*.

Some Hiftories fpeak of ftrange *Extafies* of
confeffed Wiches. *R. B.* of the kingdom of
darknefs. *p.* 69, 70. Tells us of a Woman confeffing her felf a Witch, who pretended fhe had
been turned into a Wolf & killed Sheep & Cow
in that fhape, and the Cow & Sheep were killed
at that time. And of a man Wolf that was fufpected

pected in that shape, to devour Cattle, and his
face had several scratches and hurts, which they
said were given him by the Dogs that took him
for a Wolf, and he confest himself, that twice
a year he was changed from a man to a Wolf.
But this change could not be real, but an abuse
of Phantasie, either from a distracting Melancholy called *Lycanthropia*, whereby he imagined
he was transformed into a Wolf. Or else, if
he were indeed a Wizzard, the Devil cast him
into a profound trance, whereby he imagined
he was killing Cattle as a Wolf; while the mischief done was other-wise, and probably by a
real Wolf.

But those that have been obsessed have had
strange *Extasies*; as some of our afflicted persons have had their trance-fits; in which they
lay long time in a Swound, and when they
came out of them declared they had been carried to delectable places, and had seen glorious
sights of Men and Angels; as is in part declared
above, *Chapt.* 5. So that its easier to find a person possessed or distracted by such *Extasies*, than
to prove a person hereby in voluntary league
with the Devil.

17. I come next to consider the testimony
of such as confessing themselves to be Witches,
do witness against others as partners with them
in the same crime. This hath been accounted
sufficient proof by the *Common Law*. See *Keeble*.

Ibidem. And *Glanvil. Ibidem, p* 141. *&c.* The ground of it is from the received *Maxim,* That *Socii criminis,* partners in a crime, confessing their own guilt, and discovering their companions, are fit and sufficient witnesses against those their companions. As is frequently proved in cases of Murder, Treason, Robbery, Theft *&c.* and why not as well in Witchcraft ? *Perkins* makes this only a presumption. But *Bernard* makes it a convictive evidence, when one or more fellow-Witches, confessing their own Witchcraft, and bearing witness against others ; if they can make good the truth of their witness, and give sufficient proof of it : As that they have seen them with their Spirits ; ... or that they have been together in their meetings, and such like. Now in the Examinations and tryals at *Salem,* there was great plenty of this kind of Testimony ; for about Fitty confessing, they most of them if not all accused others as partners with them at their Witch meetings ; as at a great Pond nigh *Andover,* some of them said, they met together, and some at *Newbury falls,* and were Baptized there by *Satan.* And some at *Salem* Vill Spe as above shewed, *Chap.* 2. & 3. Some said, they stole an horse and rode upon it in the air from *Andover* to *Salem* Prison, and there through the grate discoursed with one whom they accused. Another declared that she with widow *S,* went to Capt. *W.* and she said *S.* gave him a blow with a great stick,

ſtick, and yet were to him inviſible : Capt. *W.*
declared he had a ſore blow as if with a great
ſtick, but ſaw no body.   Widow *S.* denyed
that ſhe ſtruck him ; then *M. G.* the confeſſor
very boldly looked up in her face, and ſaid,
G. S. you know you did ſtrike him, and I ſaw
you do it, and then told the manner how it
was done, and how they came to him and returned.   There were many ſuch inſtances
which ſeemed exceeding demonſtrative in that
day.   Yet upon an after review of the whole
theſe confeſſors teſtimony appeareth to be very
doubtful, if not utterly falſe.   Yet I would not
deny all evidence of confeſſors to be rejected :
for the caſe may be ſo that perſons may give
ſuch infallible ſigns of their own guilt of this,
(as well as other crimes) and ſuch tokens of
real repentance for the ſame, as may render
their teſtimony notwithſtanding their former
tranſgreſſion as credible, as the teſtimony of
any other confeſſing Malefactor.   As *Manaſſeh*
who uſed Witchcraft, and dealt with a familiar
Spirit ; *and afterward beſought the Lord & hum-*
bled himſelf greatly &c. 2 *Chron.* 33. 6, 12, 13.
Was as fit (had he been a Subject) to be a
competent witneſs in any Court of Judicature,
againſt thoſe that had been partners with him
in thoſe abominations, as any other man.

Here we muſt diſtinguiſh between *Penitent*
Confeſſors, and *Impenitent Magicians.*

If a *Magician* or white Witch (as they are
called)

called) come in to difcover and teftify againft
another to be a Witch; *This (as* Perkins *faith,*
Chap. 7. *p.* 2 • 9.) *is no more then the Devils tefti-*
mony, becaufe by the Devils help he revealeth the
Witch. And indeed fuch are but the Devils
tools to do his work at his beck, and fo will as
readily accufe the innocent as the guilty. But
the reafons that fway with me to queftion the
truth of the confeffors, *Anno* 1692 notwith-
ftanding their feeming repentance for fuch
crimes, are fuch as thefe.

1. Thefe confeffors by their plaufible confeffions and accufations of others begetting credit, have been a great if not the greateft Engine
of Satan to carry on the accufing and apprehending of others, until this matter came to fuch
an height, that if it had not been ftopped might
have brought the beft Chriftians in the Country, under the imputation of that abomination,
and have involved all in confufion or blood.
The kingdom of Satan being fo evident in the
winding up of that whole contrivance, leads us
to fee his finger in this principal means, for the
managment of it.

2. Some of thefe confeffors were firft under
diabolical vexations, (as the other afflicted or
obfeffed perfons were) and under thofe torments did, as they fay, fign to a Book prefented to them, real or imaginary, by which they
obtained eafe of their pains: And then Satan in
their fhapes afflicted others who accufed them
until

until they confeffed. And after fuch confeffions againft themfelves, they alfo accufed others,
as being with them, and they were afflicted
themfelves, as they had been at the firft and
complained againft their Neighbours as others
did. So that thefe perfons may juftly be
efteemed *Dæmonizomenoi*, under fome kind of
obfeffion and delufion of Satan all this time,
and fo their Phantafies and Sences abufed by
him all the while; Satan fometimes tearing of
them as a devouring Lyon, and at other times
beguiling of them, as a Subtil Serpent.

3. Others that were not fo afflicted before
their Confeffing, were fo, prefently after it,
and fo may be reckoned in the fame predica-
ment with the others.

4. I am jealous, and I hope with a godly
jealoufie, that fome by thefe their accufations of
others, hoped to gain time and get favour from
the Rulers. And that fome of the inferiour
fort of people did ill Offices, by promifing
them favour thereby more than they had
ground to engage. And that fome under
thefe temptations regarded not as they fhould
what became of others, fo that they could
thereby ferve their own turns. And I have
been credibly informed, that fome have fince
acknowledged fo much.

5. Thefe Confeffors fince deny their Confeffions, and accufing of others, or fay they remember nothing of what they faid or did in
that

that day, whether truly or not, will be more
manifest another day. We may then well
question the validity of those Testimonies
which the Testifiers themselves do not stand
to justify now the scean is changed.

18. I come in the next place to consider a
persons evidence against him or her self by
their Confession upon examination and tryal.
This is by Scripture declared to be sufficient
Evidence against persons *Compotes mentis,* of a
sound understanding, *Luk.* 19. 22. *Out of thine
own mouth will I condemn, or judge thee.* Yea,
sufficient to justify an Execution upon it, whether the person speak truly or not. As *David*
said to the *Amalekite* that affirmed he had killed *Saul.* Thy mouth hath testified against
thee, 2 *Sam.* 1. 16. Yet its very probable that
Saul slew himself without the help of any o-
ther. 1 *Sam.* 31. 4, 5. But there have been ex-
cepted, self-accusers when distracted, demoniacks, Lunatick, under witted, over watched, and
persons surprized upon sudden fear or hope of
favour to be thereby gained, So that we may
hope some of those at *Salem* belied themselves.

1. Those that being grievously vexed with
the Devil did, and said they well understood
not what themselves. As above said.

2. It's probable, some being accused, and
their own Relations among others, suspecting
them, and vehemently urging them to confess
                                                                them;

themselves guilty, were so surprized and amazed, that they confessed that in their haste,
which they have cause to repent at leisure.
And having once accused themselves, they
feared to retract it presently, left a worse thing
should come upon them. But since they have
recanted, those Confessions, and some such
there were, whose conversations before and
since that day have been sober and blameless,
and give cause to hope better things of them.

. 3. But there were others, whose Confessions
seemed more free and demonstrative of reality, and some who confessed upon real or pretended horrour of Conscience ; and these attended with such circumstances, that some will
say, there is no believing mankind confessing
their guilt of any Crime, if these must not be
believed. But I leave the true state of their
case, to a farther discovery, when the Lord
please, in this life, or when God shall Judge the
secrets of men.

CHAPTER XIII.

HAving spoken of many supposed presumptions to discover a Witch, and shewed
the invalidity of them. I shall enquire what
is meant by a Witch. *Exod. 22. 18.* For the clearing whereof, I shall enquire who are the Cri-
minals condemned, *Deut.* 18. 10, 11. Concerning whom.

1. Ob-

1. Obferve, That they were all Heathens, who being ignorant of the true God, worfhipped the Devil inftead of God; fo that all the crimes there condemned, are crimes which fo far as they related to any Deity, refpected the Devil as their God.

2. That all the nine crimes there condemned were of a like nature in general, and are either divers names for the fame thing, or fet forth fins very like one to another. (1.) This appeareth in the frequent putting of fundry of them together, when they are prohibited or condemned, as, *Lev.* 19. 31. & 20. 6, 31. *The Wizard, and him that hath a familiar fpirit* are condemned together; and *Mic.* 5. 12. *Witch-crafts and Soothfayers.* And *Jer.* 27. 9. *Diviners, Dreamers, Enchanters and Sorcerers*, that is Witches, are put together. *Dan.* 2. 2, 27. *Magicians, Sorcerers, Aftrologers, Soothfayers* are conjoyned. So, *Ifa.* 47. 9, 12, 13. & 1 *Sam.* 28. 3, 8, 9. *Ifa.* 8. 19. & 19. 3. (2.) The fame perfons are frequently charged with the guilt of the abominations, fignified by feveral of thefe names together. As *Manaffeh* is charged with fix of thefe abominations. *2 Chron.* 33. 6. *viz. Caufing his children to pafs thorow the fire, obferving times, ufing Enchantments, ufing Witchcrafts, dealing with a familiar fpirit, dealing with Wizards.* *Ahaz* is charged. *2 Chron.* 28. 3. with the firft of thefe. The ten Tribes are charged with three of thefe abominations, *2 King.* 17. 17.

17. *viz. Divination, Enchantments, and causing their Children to pass through the fire.* (3.) Sundry of these crimes are ranked with the gross Idolatrous worshipping of false Gods of the Apostates from the true God in *Israel.* As *Manasseh*, is charged with worshipping *Baalim* and the Host of Heaven, and then with observing times, *&c.* 2 *Chron.* 33. 2, 3, 5, 6. So *A-baz*, 2 *Chron.* 28. 3,4,23,25. So the ten Tribes. 2 *King.* 17. 7, 8, 11, 12, 16, 17. And *Judah*, *Isa.* 2. 6, 7, 8, 9. They are said to be like the *Philistins* in Soothsayings, and worship *Idols*, *&c.* See *Psal.* 106. 35, 36, 37, 38. 2 *King.* 23. 5, 8, 10, 12, 13, 24. (4.) There seems then in all these abominations to be some idolatrous worship of the Heathen Gods, that is the Devil, whereby some special service was done to him; and that in expectation of some great good or benefit they expected to receive from him thereby. So the *Egyptians* in their distress sought to the Idols, Charmers, Wizards, and to them, that had familiar spirits. *Isa.* 19. 3. That is that by those persons and means they might implore and obtain the assistance of their Gods, to deliver them from the calamities felt or feared.

1. The first then is making thy *Son to pass through the Fire*; that is to *Moloch*, or any false God, forbidden & condemned, *Lev* 18. 21. *&* 20. 2. The sin of *Ahaz.* 2 *King.* 16 3. and of *Manasseh.* 2 *King.* 21. 6. *who observed times, used inchantments,*

inchantments, dealt with familiar spirits and Wiz-
ards, and used Witchcrafts 2 *Chron* 33. 6. So that
we may observe this iniquity hath some affinity with Witchcraft and the sins mentioned,
Deut. 18. 10, 11. partly because joyned with
them in this place ; and also because this and
Manassehs Witchcrafts, &c are joyned together
in the places above-mentioned. And this sin
is also reckoned with the Divinations and Enchantments of the Ten *Tribes* 2 *King* 17. 17,
30, 31. *Judah* fell to it. This iniquity was a
solemn dedication, or sacrificing their Sons and
Daughters to the Devil, *Psal.* 106 37. though
under the name of a God, as of *Moloch*, *Lev.*
20. 2. or some other false Gods. *Deut.* 12 30,
31. And this Dedication was as the Ancients
describe it, of two kinds.

1. By burning their Children to death in the
Fire, as a Sacrifice to the Devil ; which seems
to be signified by the burning in the fire, *Deu.*
12 31. *& Psal.* 106. 37, 38. *For they shed the*
innocent blood of their children. So the *Grecians*
sacrificed to *Diana, Agamemnons* Daughter, to
procure a good Wind for their Fleet. *Ovid*
Metamorphosis, lib. 13 This Sacrificing by the
apostate *Jews*, in *Jeremiah's* time, was in *To-*
phet, in the Valley of the Son of *Hinnom. Jer.*
7. 31. *&* 19. 5, 6 From hence it is that Hell
is called in the Greek, *Geenna. Mat.* 5. 22, 29,
30. From the hebrew *Gehinnom*, *& Tophet. Isa.*
30. 33. God hereby shewing the detestation
he

he had of their Idolatry and Cruelty in thofe Sacrifices.

2. There was another fort of paffing thro' the Fire; when the Child paffed between two fires, as a folemn dedication of him to that falfe God they facrificed unto. This probably was *Manaffeh's* fin, *2 Chron.* 33. 6. For it's faid, *he caufed his children to pafs thorow the fire.* But he did not facrifice to death all his Children; Though he might by fuch a dedication, confecrate them to the hoft of Heaven, or to the Heathen Gods. By either or both thefe ways, fuch Idolaters did make or confirm a Covenant with the Devil by facrifice. As Gods people did make a Covenant with God, by, facrificing to him, *Pfal.* 50. 5. And did thereby fhew their feeking help from the Devil, their invocation of him, and dependance upon him for fome great things they fuppofed he could fupply them with. So that here was one kind of charming or inchantment ufed to a falfe God, which was condemned to death. *Exod.* 22. 20. For by the ufing thefe abominable Ceremonies, they did invocate the Devil to do them fome great good. As the *Græcians* facrificed *Agamemnons* Daughter to procure a Wind for their Navy, and having a fair Wind, afterwards imputed it unto their Sacrifice. And by that Law, *Lev.* 20. 2, 3. *He that giveth any of his feed to* Moloch, *fhall furely be put to death.* Thefe Sacrificers in *Ifrael*, ought to dye.

2. The

2. The second Sin foretold, *Deut.* 18. 10. is, That useth Divination. *Kosem Kesaamim* in Hebrew, from the verb *Kasam*, to divine, which is in its derivatives sometimes used in a good sence. *Prov.* 16. 10. *Isa.* 3. 2. *Kosem*, The prudent. But *Deut.* 18. 10. used in an evil sence. And *Ezek.* 12. 24. for a flattering divination; such was *Balaam*, Josh. 13. 22. A *soothsayer*, or diviner: the *Philistine Priests*, 1 *Sam.* 6. 2. *Judahs* false Prophets, *Ezek.* 13. 6, 7, 23. *Jer.* 14. 14. *Ezek.* 22. 28. *Micah* 3. 6, 11. *Zech.* 10. 2. *Jer.* 29. 8. Though they prophecied in the Name of the Lord : but false & vain visions. Applyed also to the *Babylonish* Priests, *Ezek.* 24. 21. 23. and to their diviners, *Isa.* 44. 25. And *Sauls* rebellion is compared to the sin of Witchcraft, 1 *Sam.* 15. 23. Or of *Kosem*, that is divination, which shews it was a great sin : whether the divining were by, or in the Name of the true God, or a false God : And it was a prophecying of things to come true or false, or using means whereby they might fore-know future contingencies, and so be able to foretel them, as *Ezek.* 21. 21, 23.

3. Is an observer of times. *Hebr. Megnonen.* Always used to shew a wicked practice, as 2 *Chron.* 33. 6. Tis one of the sins of *Manasseh.* Tis forbidden, *Lev.* 19. 26. *Neither shall ye observe times.* A sin of the *Philistines*, imitated by the wicked Jews, *Isa* 2. 6. there translated *Soothsayers* : and from this, some of them are called, *Sons*

Sons of the Sorceress, I*sai.* 57. 2. Of *Gnonenabi*
A sin of the *Amonites, Moabites,* and other heathens condemned, *Jer.* 27 3, 9, 10. translated
Enchanters ; when they prophecyed a lye to
them ; *saying, ye shall not serve the King of Babylon.* Some of the Hebrew Doctors derive the
word from *Gnajin,* an eye, and interpret it of
them that hold and abuse the eyes, so as to
make men think, they see what is not really so.
Some others derive it from *Gnanan,* a cloud, &
hold it to be a kind of divining by the clouds.
And others from *Gnon,* time, who by their pretended skill foretel what times are good, or evil
to attend any weighty business in. Such are
called *Soothsayers, Micah* 5. 12 *And observer of
times, Deut.* 18. 14. The Greek translation
('which was before the birth of Christ) call
him *Cledonizomenos* ; a foreteller of things to
come, or a fortune-teller.

4. Name is an *Enchanter. Menachesh* of the
verb *Nichesh,* which is used in a lawful sence,
Gen. 30. 27. *I have learned by experience.* And
of *Joseph* divining by his cup, *Gen* 44 5, 15.
Which *Ainsworth* rendereth, *searching, search diligently* (that is) by this cup : Or (as it may
be translated) make tryal of you ; that is, whether you are such men as you profess your
selves to be. And indeed by this cup in *Ben-
jamins* sack did *Joseph* try and search out his
brethren, to prove what love they did bear to
their father *Jacob* and brother *Benjamin,* which

I underſtand to be the divining of *Joſeph* there intended. But moſtly the word is uſed to ſignify ſome wicked practice : As for the enchantments of *Balaam*, *Numb*. 24. 1. & 23. 23. Of *Manaſſeh*, 2 *Chron* 33.6. Of the ten tribes, 2 *King*. 17. 17. And is condemned, *Lev*. 19 26.

5. Abomination is a *Witch*. *Mechaſheph* Note this word is always uſed to ſet forth ſome wicked abomination, and the worker of it. The *Egyptian* ſorcerers are charged with it, *Exod*. 7. 11. Who are called Sorcerers, or Witches. *Mechaſhepim* And *Manaſſeh*, 2 *Chron*. 33 6. uſed *Witchcraft* : and the wiſe men of *Babylon*, that *Nebucadnezer* ſent for to tell and interpret his dream, are called, *Dan*. 2. 2. *Mechaſhepim Witches*, or as tis tranſlated *Sorcerers*. Such alſo were the Prophets of the *Edomites* and heathen Nations, *Jer*. 27. 9. called there *Sorcerers*. And the *Babylonians* are charged as guilty of Witchcrafts, called *Sorcerys*, *Iſa* 47. 9, 12. And *Niniveh* is called a Miſtreſs of Witchcrafts, *Nahum*. 3 4. And *Jezabel* is charged by *Jehu* with this wickedneſs, 2 *King* 9. 22. And *Judah* alſo is charged with this abomination, *Micah* 5. 12. Yea after their return from *Babylon*, *Mal*. 3. 5. Where the Lord threatens to be a ſwift witneſs againſt the Sorcerers, or witches among them. The *Septuagint* Greek tranſlation render this word, which is by us called in the Scripture *Witch* and *Sorcerer*, by the name *Pharmacos*, and their Witchcrafts and Sorcerys, they call *Phar-*
maca

maca and *Pharmaceia* : and so these Greek
names are in the New-Testament translated,
(which very much follows this Greek translation in quoting the Scriptures of the old Testa-
ment) *Gal.* 5. 20. *Witchcraft, Sorcerys, Rev.* 9.
21.&18. 23. And *Sorcerers, Rev.*21. 8. & 22.15.

6. The sixth inquiry here condemned is,
A Charmer. Hebr. Chobe Chaber ; a Charmer of
Charms: of *Chaber*,to joyn together in Society.
Sometimes used for a lawful *Associating* ; but in
Deuteronomy & other places, for a wicked joyn-
ing Society, as *Isa.* 47. 9, 12. translated *Enchant-
ment : stand now to thine Enchantments, &c.*
And *Psal.* 58. 5. used to express the Charming
of a Serpent. The Greek call such an one,
Epaidan Epaioden : the Charmer of a Charm.

7. The seventh word is, *A consulter with familiar Spirits.* Hebr. its *Shoel Ob,* that asketh of
Ob,the familiarSpirit ; rendred by *Buxtorf,Pytho,*
a sin forbidden,*Lev* 19,31. So that the regarding
those that have familiarSpirits is prohibited,*Lev.*
19 31.& *Lev.* 20. 27. The man or woman that
hath *Ob,* that is, a familiar Spirit, shall be put
to death. See *Lev.* 20 6 This was one of *Manassehs* sins, 2 *Chron* 33 6. 2 *King.* 21. 6. And
for going to such a Woman, the Lord killed
Saul, 1 *Chron.* 10. 13. See of these, *Isa.* 8 19.
& 19. 3 & 29. 4. Such as these are commonly joyned with Wizards,as in the Scriptures
quoted. And such *Saul* cut off, 1 *Sam.* 28.3,9.
and yet after that sought to such an one to his

own deſtruction, 1 Sam 28 7, to 21. namely to the Witch at Endor. The Greek tranſlators in the Scriptures above quoted, call them, Eg-gaſtrimuthai: pe ſons that ſpeak in or from their bellies, becauſe of old time as Hiſtories mentioned, thoſe who prophecyed or ſpake by inſpiration of the Devil, or heathen Gods, ſpake as from their bellies, when they gave anſwers to the people from their heathen oracles. Which probably is pointed at, Iſa. 8. 19. Where ſuch are ſaid to *peep and mutter*; and Iſa 29 4. *To ſpeak out of the ground, and out of the duſt.*

8　The Eighth name for theſe abominable perſons is, A Wizard. Hebr. *Jiddegnoni*; of *Jadang to know*. But here notes ſuch an art and way of knowing as is wicked, not allowed of by God, and therefore not proceeding from nature, or lawful art, or divine Revelation; therefore from Satan. Such are condemned as worthy of death. *Lev* 20. 27 And it was one of the Iniquities of *Manaſſeh*, 2 *Chron* 33. 6. *He dealt with Wizards. Gnaſhah Jiddegnoni*; He prepared, obtained or made uſe of Wizards. This name is commonly joyned with the having familiar ſpirits; as, *Levit* 19 31 & 20. 6, 27 1 *Sam.* 28. 39. 2 *King.* 9. 21. 6. & 23. 24. *Iſa*. 8. 19 & 19. 3. So that it ſeems to be another name to ſignifie one that hath a familiar ſpirit, for his knowledge thereby, or at leaſt to agree in the main with ſuch.

9　Name is, A *Necromancer, Doreſh El. Hammetbim,*

methim, a *Seeker to the Dead*. This was the sin
of the Witch at *Endor* to seek unto dead *Samuel* to give counsel to living *Saul*, 1 *Sam*. 28.
which is also condemned. *Isa* 8. 19 *Should a
people seek for the living to the dead?* This opinion was among the Heathen, that the Dead
might be raised, and give them advice. So
Pomphey in his distress desired the Ghost of a
dead Souldier might come to him, to give him
counsel what to do. And by such means, the
Devil counterfeiting himself, this or that dead
person, often deceived them And by such
kind of Apparitions, the Doctrine of Purgatory, and other Superstitions have been much
rivetted among the vulgar with the Papists. By
viewing the crimes condemned, *Deut*. 18. 10,
11. as they are mentioned in other Scriptures,
we shall find, they all speak of sins very like
one to another, and some of them but divers
names for the same crime. The Lord aim-
ing in this place to condemn all those diabolical Artists, by whatever names they were known
among the *Israelites*, or *Canaanites*. For we
shall find several of these names fixed upon the
same person, as on *Manasseh*, 2 *Chron*. 33 6.
Six of these names, or crimes are fastened upon
him. And the Witch at *Endor* is mentioned,
1 *Sam*. 28. as one that was a *Necromancer*, a
Wizard, and having a familiar spirit, and a Diviner by it. See also, *Isa*. 47. 9 12, 13. *Jer*.
27. 9. Hence then the way to understand the

crimes

crimes pointed at in the prohibitions mentioned in *Deut*. 18. is to examine what were the
crimes those stand charged with in Scripture
who are branded with any of these names.

I begin with the Sorcerers or Witches of
Egypt, *Exod.* 7. These did imitate the real
Miracles of *Moses*, in making frogs, and turning his Staff into a Serpent, and water into
blood : And this was done by these Sorcerers,
either by some humane power, art and dexterity, or by the assistance of the Gods of Egypt
(mentioned, *Numb*. 33. 4. 2 *Sam*. 7. 23.)
that is by the Devils aid. But they could not
do these things by humane power, art, or dexterity ; therefore by the Egyptian Gods. *i.e.*
the Devils. This will appear, if we consider
what was the case between *Moses* and *Pharaoh*,
and why *Pharaoh* sent for his Sorcerers. *Moses*
by the Lords commission said to *Pharaoh*, *Exo.*
5. 1. *And the Lord* (or Jehovah, for so it is in
Hebrew) *the God of Israel saith, Let my people
go, &c. Pharaoh* answered, *Who is Jehovah that
I should obey his voice?* As if he had said, I
know not this Jehovah, I worship other Gods,
even the Gods of *Egypt*. Now then *Moses*
must prove Jehovah ought to be obeyed, and
that must be by working a Miracle as a sign
to *Pharaoh*. This *Pharaoh* asketh of *Moses*, and
God promiseth that he will do for and by *Mo-*
ses, Exod. 7. 3, 5, 9. The case between *Pharaoh*
and *Moses*, was somewhat like the case between

tween *Eliah* and *Baals* Prophets. 1 *King.* 18. *Whose God should be worshipped?* and this muft be tryed by fome fign, as here by frogs, lice, locufts, &c. So there by fire fetcht from Heaven to confume the Sacrifice; and in both cafes, the Lord fhews he is greater than all Gods, as *Jethro* acknowledged; *For in the thing wherein they dealt proudly, the Lord was above them.* In profecution of this Commiffion, *Mofes* and *Aaron* turn their Rod into a Serpent, and the water of *Egypt* into blood, and bring frogs to cover the land of *Egypt* : Here were real Miracles, which prove that Jehovah ought to be obeyed. For that Meffage which is confirmed by evident Miracles, comes from the God of Power and Truth, and therefore ought to be obeyed. *Pharoah* now will try if his Sorcerers cannot do as much as *Mofes* and *Aaron,* that he may invalidate the Miracles of *Mofes,* and it's faid, *they did in like manner, Exo.* 7. 11, 12, 22. & 8. 7. *Gnafhafhu Chen.* They did fomewhat like to what *Aaron* had done. If it were by humane power and dexterity only, then it muft be by bringing Serpents, Blood and Frogs under their garments, or the like, and by flight of hand, flipping them down before the company with fuch celerity, that the things firft prefented, might feem to be transformed into another nature. But that it was not fo appears,

1. In that they could not be provided before

fore hand with Serpents, blood and frogs, to
present before *Pharoah* at those times, because
no humane art could tell them before-hand,
what Miracles *Aaron* would work, to inable
them to stock themselves with such provision
before hand.

2. Had they so done by meer humane art,
there had been no comparison between the actings of *Moses* and theirs; and so no argument
to direct whose God was to be obeyed, whether Jehovah, or the Gods of *Egypt* . For *Pharoah* and his Courtiers, yea, and *Moses* also
could easily discover such legerdemain, and
indeed it would have rendred the Magicians
ridiculous, and *Pharoah* for improving of them.
For *Pharoah* was convicted that what *Aaron*
did was a reality ; *for* Aarons *rod deveured the
Magicians rods, and the blood was so over all the
land of Egypt, that the fish died, and the River
stank, and the Egyptians wanted drink, and the
frogs so covered the Land of Egypt, that* Pharoah
*acknowledged they came by Jehovah. For he re-
questeth* Moses *and* Aaron *to intreat Jehovah to
take the frogs away,* Chap. 8. 8.

3. If they had only brought Serpents, Frogs,
&c. from other places, and thrown them down
by jugling slight of hand ; then when *Aaron*
brought lice upon man, and beast, they could
have taken lice also, and scattered them about ;
for they tryed by their inchantments to bring
forth lice, but could not : and yet lice
were

were as easily, if not more easily obtained than
frogs and serpents, and they were men still,
and had their hands and feet to act with now
as well as before: But now they are convinced
and confess, This is the finger of God; that is
of a greater God than any we worship and
work by.

4. The Magicians brought frogs up upon
the land of *Egypt. ver. 7* which shews they
produced frogs in more places than just where
they stood and acted; and therefore did not
act meerly by slight of hand.

Hence we may conclude, that the Serpents,
Blood, and Frogs the Magicians shewed, were
effects above mans power, and not by Jehovah, therefore by the Devil, the God of *Egypt.*
Whether the Devil did only delude the sight,
and bewitch the eyes of *Pharoah,* and the *Egyptians,* or make real frogs and serpents out of
the putrid matter in *Egypt,* or make aerial bodies like them, or that it was the Devils assu-
ming such like shapes, I determine not: But
we may observe, that here the Devil, and his
Magicians went very far, and farther than at
other times; for now *Moses* is at hand to overcome their delusions by the power of Jehovah,
and to convince beholders, that there is no
God of the Heathen, can work like the God
of *Israel.* Yet for a time the true Miracles of
Moses, and the seeming ones of the Magicians
seem to be pretty much alike. For it's said,
they

*they cast down every man his rod, and they be-
came* Serpents. It is not said, & they ſhuffled in
Serpents inſtead of their rods, but their rods
were ſerpents, at leaſt in outward appearance.
Theſe effects then ſo like to *Moſes* real Miracles, might move the Magicians to try a fourth
time if they could not by their inchantments
produce lice, but here their power failed. And
the true reaſon was, their God was in chains,
and the Lord bound him that he ſhould proceed no further to delude men by his pretended miraculous power.

2. *I Enquire what was the Crime of the
Woman at* Endor, *that had a familiar ſpirit ?*
I Sam. 28. 7, *&c.*

A. She was ſuch an one as *Saul* had cut off
as being a Wizard, and having a familiar ſpirit. *ver.* 3. *&* 9. In hebrew they are called,
Eſh Haobeth ; that is, thoſe that have *Ob.* and
ver. 7. *Eſheth bagnalath Ob.* A woman that is
miſtreſs of *Ob.* that is rendred one that is Miſtreſs of *Pytho,* a Prophecying Spirit. *Eng-
gaſtrimuthai* as above declared ; one that ſpeaks
as from her belly by help of the Devil.

Q. *What then was this* Pytho, *or* Ob ?

A. It was a divining ſpirit ; to divine by
the Devil. Whence the poſſeſſed Damoſel,
Acts 16. 16. is ſaid to have the ſpirit of *Pytho,*
which was the Devil that poſſeſſed her, by
whom ſhe did *Sootbſay.* The Jewiſh Rabbi,
Aben Eſra ſaith, they were called *Ob,* becauſe
from

from a belly fwelled like a bottle, they gave
out their Oracles. And *Oboth* is tranflated
bottles, *Job* 32. 19. *Ainfworth* on *Deut.* 18. 11.
faith, fuch Magicians are fo called, becaufe
they fpeak with an hollow voice as out of a
bottle.

This Woman at *Endor* was then one that
only plaid tricks with a bottle, or one that
was miftrefs of *Ob* the Devil as her familiar
fpirit to wait upon her ; not the former, therefore the latter. For (1.) By this her Spirit, fhe
offers to bring up to *Saul* whom he defired: *v.*
11. (2.) She brings up the fuppofed *Samuel*,
(*i.e.* as I conceive, the Devil in *Samuels* likenefs) That doth fo much refemble *Samuel* for
his Age, Complexion, Mantle and Voice, that
Saul takes him to be real *Samuel* : And makes
anfwer to him as if he were the real *Samuel.*
ver. 15. And receives a fad meffage from him,
as if it had been fpoken by *Samuel* himfelf.
ver. 16, 17, 18, 19. So that this Woman was
a Necromancer in raifing up dead *Samuel*, or
the Devil in his likenefs. Some indeed do
plead that this woman only plaid tricks with a
bottle, and a cunning knave affifting of her,
counterfeited the voice of *Samuel*, and deceived *Saul* thereby. And they plead that *Oboth* is
in one place tranflated bottles, *viz. Job* 32.
19. Whether truly or not, I now ftay not to
difcufs ; but if it were truly tranflated fo here,
yet in fourteen other places, *Ob.* and *Oboth* is
tranfla-

tranſlated a familiar ſpirit, or ſpirits; and we
are to compare this in 1 *Sam.* 28. with thoſe
many Scriptures where it's rendred ſo as referring to an Evil Spirit.

But ſay they *Manaſſeh,* 2 *Chron.* 33. 6. dealt
with a familiar ſpirit : hebrew, 'tis *Gnaſhah Ob.*
which they would render he made *Ob.* Now
ſay they he could not make a familiar ſpirit,
although he might a bottle.

To which I anſwer.

1. The verb *Gnaſhah,* ſignifies to get, obtain,
or ſet up (as the *Dutch* tranſlate it) ſo that
here is nothing in this place to make for their
turn; for though he could not make a familiar ſpirit, yet he could obtain, or ſet up a familiar ſpirit.

2 *Manaſſeh* his ſin in this was like his Sacrificing his Children through the fire, which was
certainly a kind of invocation of a falſe God, *i. e.*
the Devil; and the deſcription of his apoſtaſy,
v. 3 *to* 8 ſhews that he was turned from the
true God to the Gods of the heathen, to worſhip, and invocate them, and why not to have
a ſpirit to obtain anſwers by, called *Ob* ? But
that this Witch at *Endor* did more than play
tricks with a bottle, appeareth. (1) Becauſe her
ſin was a capital crime, and they that ſought to
ſuch perſons were curſed of God, *Lev.* 19 31.
& 20 6, 27. *Iſa.* 8. 19. And it cannot be apprehended that ſhe and others would hazzard
their lives meerly to play tricks with a bottle,

or

or that the people heathens and *Israelites* should
be so exceedingly addicted to follow such, as to
need such severe prohibitions, and punishments
therefore. (2.) *Saul* had put many such to
death for having *Ob* : And its not likely this
woman after this would keep such a bottle to
play with to the hazard of her life. (3) *Saul*
and his Courtiers that had cut off so many of
them, must necessarily know what the crime
was, they were put to death for. (4) *Saul*
fought not for one that could play tricks with
a bottle ; but for one that by the help of her
familiar could raise *Samuel* (or a Spirit in his
likeness) which was agreeable to a corrupt o-
pinion among them, that they might seek help
from the dead : forbidden *Isa.* 8 19. *Should a
people seek for the living to the dead*, i. e. *to the
Souls of the Dead.* (5.) If she had only play'd
tricks with a bottle, how could she or any other
personate *Samuel*, as he did speaking to *Saul*,
v. 15, 16, 17, 18, 19 ? If it be said, she had a
man, a knave, to come in such a garb to personate the voice & mantle of *Samuel* : Then I
ask, how in the night time this woman without
notice given could have a counterfeiting knave
and mantle in such a readiness ? For *Saul* came
to her in the night & without warning, *v.* 8, 9.
(6) A meer juggling knave or quean could not
prophecy the victory of the *Philistians*, the
death of *Saul* and his Sons, *Jonathan* and the
rest, as the supposed *Samuel* did, But Satan
might

might so know and prophesy (as I may farther
shew hereafter.)   For *Saul* dyed for this very
sin, in going to ask counsel of one that had a familiar Spirit, to enquire of it,   1 *Chron.* 10. 13,
14.   And this the Lord might discover to Satan
for the punishment of *Saul*, as he did the death
of *Ahab* unto Satan, upon a like account.   As
Micaiah was shewed in a vision,   1 *King.* 22. 19,
to 23.

3. I enquire, *What was the profession & practice
of the* Babylonian *Sorcerers mentioned,* Isa. 47. 9,
12, 13, 14 *Ezek.* 21. 21. *Dan.* 2. 2.

A. 1. They were like the Sorcerers of E-
gypt, for they have the same general names of
Sorcerers and wise men.

2. They were *Chotsim bacochabim* ; that is,
Prophets by the Stars : (translated *Stargazers*)
for *Chotseh* is used to signify a Prophet, or Seer.
Isa. 30. 10. 2 *Sam.* 24. 11. 1 *Chorn.* 21. 9. & 25.
5. 2 *Chron.* 9. 29 & 12. 15. & 19. 2. & 29. 26.
& 35. 15. *Amos* 7. 12   Here are ten times or
places where this word is used to signify a Prophet ; which give light unto this place, to shew
that these Stargazers did prophesy by the Stars.
And it cannot be understood of any foretelling
by them, of signs, seasons, days & years, which
God ordained them for, *Gen.* 1. 14. For that is
a knowledge lawful and commendable, and at-
tainable by lawful art & study : but what the
Prophet chargeth them with here was unlawful,
and therefore such a kind of prophecying, as
pro-

proceeded from a falſe God, that is the Devil.

3. They are called *Monthly Prognoſticators.* *Modignim lechadaſhim,* knowers by the months ; *Modignim* proceeds from the ſame *Radix* with *Jiddegnoni,* a *Wizard,* and hath ſome affinity with it here.   Theſe then were a ſort of fore-tellers of things to come, by the Months or Moon.

4. Add to this, that *v.* 9. & 12. they are charged with the guilt of Sorcerys or Witch-crafts, and Inchantments, which ſhews what kind of Prophets they were.

2. They uſed Witchcraft in a way of opera-tion, whereby they endeavoured to deliver their Country from the evils coming on them. This appeareth, (1.) By the challenge *Iſaiah* makes to them, *v.* 12. *Stand now to thine inchant-ments, &c. if ſo be thou ſhalt be able to profit, if ſo be thou mayeſt prevail. q. d.* They hoped to put off the miſchief and deſolation that was to come upon them, by their Witchcrafts, *&c.* (2.) He tells them, *their Aſtrologers &c. ſhould not ſave them from the things coming on them ; but ſhould be as ſtubble and the fire ſhould burn them &c. v.* 13, 14, 15. Which intimates, that theſe Aſtrologers *&c.* did ſtrive and endeavour it with hopes to prevail ; but the Lord would o-verrule and diſappoint their endeavours.

3. Compare this with *Ezek.* 21. 21. Where their diviners uſed divinations to know ſecret futurities, *viz.* Whether they ſhould go to *Je-ruſalem*

rusalem and prosper, or to *Rabbath* and prosper. That this was a diabolical divination may be seen, if we consider. (1.) The thing they sought for was a future contingent event to man unknown. (2.) The means they use to discover this secret were, by Images or *Teraphim* (which were the Devils oracles,) and by arrowes, and by looking into the liver, for signs of direction to know which of these places they should first go to, & whether they should prosper in their way. And these means had no vertue in them to make any such discovery. (3.) Therefore they did by these rites and ceremonies invocate their gods to reveal these things to them. The Lord indeed did unknown to them over-rule the divination to that according to their Superstitious Imaginations they were inclined to go against *Jerusalem*, and God made it to prosper ; not thereby approving, or excusing their invocating false Gods : but that thereby he might use them, as the rod of his wrath against the people of his wrath. (4.) By comparing these two Scriptures above, we may see of what stamp the wise men of *Babylon* were, who were sent for by *Nebuchadnezar*, to tell and interpret his dream, *Dan.* 2. 2. And to interpret his other dream, *Dan.* 4. 6, 7. And by *Belshazzar*, to read the hand-writing and interpret, *Dan.* 5. 7. *viz.* Men that had peculiar intimacy with, and special aid from their false Gods, as the Sorcerers and diviners mentioned,

oned, *Isa.* 47. *& Ezek* 21. For (1.) They
have the same name, *Mecbasphim* Sorcerers and
Witches: and *Chartummim,*one of the names of
the Sorcerers of *Egypt, Exod.* 7. 11. (2) This
was agreeable to the end those Kings sent for
them, *viz* to discover secrets which other men
could not. And they confidently profess a
skill to interpret the Dream,if they may know
what it is. *Dan.* 2 6. Which seems to hold
forth that they depended upon a power super-
humane, to discover to them the interpretation of Dreams; yet they confess they cannot
reveal the dream it self. And good reason, for
the Gods they served knew it not. Yet they
by the Gods whose dwelling is not with flesh,
could reveal it. Which shews they acknowledge a Divine Power that knew the greatest
secrets, who is indeed the true God unknown
to them. And when *Daniel* had revealed the
Dream and its interpretation. *Dan.* 2. And afterwards interpreted another dream. *Dan.* 4.
He is acknowledged to excel all the Wise men
of *Babylon* in that,*in him was the spirit of the Holy
Gods. Dan.* 4. 8. *&* 5. 11. That is, the spirit of
a God above their Gods; a God that was as
Nebuchadnezzar confesseth, *Dan.* 2. 47. *A God
of Gods, and a Revealer of secrets.* The High
God. *Dan.* 4. 2. Yet this hinders not but that
the Magicians, *&c.* had more of the spirit of
their Gods, than others had, though not equal
to *Daniel.*

H   Q 2

Q. 2. What was the sin of the Sorcerers, &c. *of* Edom *and other Nations, for which* Jeremiah *warns them not to hearken to them?* Jer. 27. 3, 9.

A. It was a prophecying a lye unto them, in the name of their false Gods, saying to them, ye shall not serve the King of *Babylon,* which was the way to destroy them, *ver.* 10, 11. I say, in the name of false Gods : For they attended to dreams (nor to your dreamers) as a way of Revelation whereby they were perswaded so to prophesy. Dreams are either, (1.) Natural, as *Ecclef.* 5. 2. 7. *Ifa.* 29. 8. *Job* 7. 14. (2) Or Divine, as the dreams of *Nebuchadnezzar, Daniel, Joseph,* &c. Or (3) Diabolical, *Deut.* 13. 1, 2. *Zech.* 10. 2. *The Diviners have told false dreams.* But the dreams of the Sorcerers. *Jer.* 27. 9. were not Divine, nor Natural ; therefore Diabolical, and so from a false God. Here note, that Divining or Prophecying by diabolical and false dreams, is one way of Sorcery and Witchcraft : And that these false Prophets are Sorcerers, in undertaking to reveal things to come, by a false God, though what they reveal do not come to pass. They no doubt sought to their God for help in this matter, and went as far as they could. So I conceive all *Baals* four hundred and fifty Prophets, 1 *King.* 18. 26. were Sorcerers, in seeking with all earnestness to *Baal* to bring down fire from heaven (though they could not perform it) for they did all they could to ob

lige

lige the Devil to help them; but their God
wanted power, and so the wonder was not
wrought at that time. These Prophets of
Baal deserved therefore to dye by the Law.
Exod. 22. 18. and by the Law. *Deut.* 18. 20.
The Prophet that shall speak in the name of
other Gods, even that Prophet shall dy. As
also by the Law. *Exod* 22. 20. *He that sacrifi-*
ceth to any God, save unto the Lord only, he shall
be utterly destroyed: For those sacrificed to *Baal*.
But if any would thence conclude, that all the
Heathen Sacrificing Priests should be put to
death: I say, it follows not, for the Heathen
among the Heathen know no better. But
these did it in *Israel*, where they had the
means to know the true God, and professedly
endeavoured to draw men from the Lord unto *Baal*.

Q. 3. *What was the sin of the Prophets in Ju-*
dah, who are called dreamers, Jer. 29. 8. 9. *and*
said to use divination, Jer. 14. 14. Ezek. 13. 6,
7, 9. 23. *and in other Scriptures?*

A. They are not called, *Mechashepim, Witch-*
es, as the false Prophets of the Heathen; yet
they were very like them. As (1.) Both sorts
used wicked divinations. (2.) As *Jannes* and
Jambres withstood *Moses*; so these withstood
the counsel of God spoken by *Jeremiah,* Jer.
27. 3. to 11. & 29. 8, 9. (3.) The divinations of both sorts of Prophets were false, as to
the matter of them; they divined a lye. *Jer.*

27. 10. *with* 29. 8, 9. *Ezek.* 13. 6, 7. (4.) As
the Heathen diviners were guided by dreamers, which came from a lying spirit. *Jer.* 27.
9 · · Nor to the dreamers of dreams, *&c.* so
these hearkened to false dreams which they
dreamed, *Jer.* 29 8. which came by Inspira-
tion or instigation of Satan. Yet they differ-
ed in this; Those prophesied in the name of
a false God, but these prophesied a lye in the
name of the true God. So that these deserved to dye by the Law. *Deut.* 18. 20. *But the*
Prophet which shall presume to speak a word in my
name, which I have not commanded him to speak,
even that Prophet shall dye.

Q. 4. *What were the Witchcrafts Jehu charged*
Jezabel with? 2 King. 9. 22.

A. 1. Either they were some practices of
Witchcraft she used, not expresly mentioned
in Scripture; or they were her protecting and
providing for, and maintaining of *Baals* Prophets who were Witches, and her making their
cause her own; as see, 1 *Kings* 16. 31. *&* 18.
19 *&* 19 1, 2. She seems to be guilty of both,
1 *King.* 21. 25. 26. She made the Prophets of
Baal's Sin her own. As *David* is said to slay
Uriah, when he did it not in his own person;
but contrived how it should be done by others.
And we may note that one reason why the
false Prophetess in *Thyatira* is called *Jezabel,* is,
because *she called her self a Prophetess, and taught*
the people to eat things sacrificed to Idols; which
was

was thereby to commit Idolatry. So that *Ahabs Jezebel* might be one of the Devils Prophetesses among the *Israelites*, and so be guilty of Witchcrafts that way ; as a teacher of Idolatrous worshipping *Baal*. And we may note that the false Gods had their female Prophetesses and Diviners as well as Males, as we see the Witch at *Endor*.

CHAPTER. XIV.

HAving spoken of the Scripture use of those evils condemned, *Deut*. 18. 10, 11. And of the persons charged with those abominations, we may hence see who those Witches, Sorcerers, Diviners *&c.* among the Heathen were, *viz.* they were a sort of Priests and Prophets of the Heathen Gods, who had a more special dedication and approaches to them, than the ordinary sort of Heathen had, whereby they obtained or at least endeavoured to obtain special help from those Gods, who were indeed the Devils.

I. *Note*, they were reckoned among the Priests & Prophets of those Idol Gods, as 1 *Sam*. 6. 2. The *Philistians* called for their Priests and diviners. And *Jer*. 27. 9, 10. they are commanded *not to hearken to their Prophets, nor Diviners, nor Enchanters, nor Sorcerers or Witches*. So when *Josiah* put away the Priests of the false Gods, he together with them put away them that had familiar Spirits, Wizards, Teraphim

and

and Idols, 2 *King.* 23. 5,10, 24. And when the ten Tribes are condemned for their heathenish Idolatries, & Sacrificing their Children through the fire; their divinations and enchantments are reckoned with these abominations, 2 *King.* 17. 10, 11, 12, 16, 17. And the false Prophets of the *Jews* in *Chaldea*, though they prophecyed by the true God, yet prophecying falsely, are called *Diviners, Jer.* 29. 8, 9. Though they pretended a Warrant from Jehovah, because of their likeness to the heathen Prophets and diviners. So *Zech.* 10. 2. *Mich.* 3. 5,6, 7. Those Prophets are called Diviners.

2. Hence as Gods people were, to have recourse to the Lords Priests and Prophets, to seek and know the mind of God, and to obtain help from him by them, 2 *Chron.* 20. 20. *Mal.* 2. 7. 1 *King.* 22. 7. So the Devil had his Priests and prophets by whom the people did enquire, & to whom they came in difficult cases, as to the God of *Ekron*, 2 *King.* 1. 2. So *Pharaoh, Nebuchadnezzar, Belshazer &c.* Send for their wisemen and Sorcerers to consult with and help in their great cases; as the Servants of the Lord sent to their wise men, the Priests & Prophets of the most High God, to consult with & help in their difficult cases. *Note,* All the Heathens were worshippers of the Devil, 1 *Cor.* 10. 20. Yet all were not Sorcerers, diviners, soothsayers, &c. but some peculiar ones. So *Balaam* among the *Midianites*, was a Soothsayer or divi-

ner, and a Prophet, *Josh.* 13. 22. *with* 2 *Pet.*2.2.
Baal had his prophets four hundred & fifty,
1 *King.*12. 22. And the Prophets of *Egypt*,*Isa.*
19.3. are called *Charmers,Wizards &c.* to whom
they fought. As among Gods worshippers all
are not Prophets, 1 *Cor.* 12. 29.

3. As the gifts and attainments of the Lords
Prophets were differing, and so their operations, as 1 *Cor.* 12. 4, 5, 6. So Satan, who is the
god of this world, doth act like the most high,
in distributing his gifts, *&c.* to his devoted Servants. As had *Moses* and *Aaron*, the gifts of miracles, so Satan had the magicians of *Egypt* that
shall come by counterfeit or seeming miracles,
as near or like to Gods Prophets as he can.
Hath the Lord his Prophets to prophesy of
things to come ? So Satan hath in some degree
like them, who shall give a sign or a wonder
that some times shall come to pass, *Deut.* 13.1,2.
Did the Lord reveal himself to some of his
Servants by dreams ? So Satan reveals himself
to some of his prophets by dreams at some
times, as *Deut.* 13. 1. *If there arise a prophet or a*
dreamer of dreames. So the Sorcerers of the
Heathen, *Jer.* 27. 9. had their dreams or
dreamers. Did the Lord give to some the gift
of interpretating dreams, as to *Joseph* and *Da-*
niel ? So Satan had his officers that pretended
at least a skill to interpret dreams, as *Dan.* 2. 7.
Did the Lord call *Abraham* and his Priest to Sacrifice his Son *Isaac*, *Gen.* 22. 2. So Satan had
H 4   his

his Priests by whom the Heathen did Sacrifice
their Sons and Daughters to him ; and cause
them to pass through the fire, &c. *Lev.* **18. 21.**
Pfal. 106. 35, 36, 37, 38 And this may be the
reason why causing Children to pass through the
fire is so often in Scripture mentioned with
Witches and Witchcraft. Because this was one
abominable way whereby the Sorcerers Sacrificed, to their Devil gods, to implore their help.
And as the Lord did more freely & familiarly
reveal himself and his counsel to some more
than others : As to *Moses, Exod* 33. 11. *To whom
the Lord spake face to face, as a man speaketh to
his friend.* So Satan had some of these his devoted Servants, to whom he was more open &
familiar in converse. And such were those
that had a familiar Spirit to appear at their call :
as the woman at *Endor*, by her familiar Spirit
divining, brings up the counterfeit *Samuel.*
And as the people did seek unto *Moses*, & such
Prophets of the Lord as had more especial ac-
quaintance with the Lord. So the heathen did
seek unto those that had these familiar Spirits,
as persons that had more especial intimacy with
their gods than themselves had. Hereupon
the* Lord strictly forbids the *Israelites* seeking
unto such, *Lev.* 19. 31. & 20. 6. *Isa.* 8. 19.

And from this intimacy between the Magicians and their god, and Satan their god, being
as it were, at their call or beck ; she that had
a familiar Spirit is called *Bagnalath Ob*, 1 *Sam.*
28.

28. 7. rendred, that hath a familiar Spirit, but it signifies a mistress of *Ob*: The spirit being subservient to the Witch, as if she were his mistress.

And hereupon it is that Writers speak of Witches being in Covenant with Satan, explicit or implicit; because Satan is so ready to act at the call of a Witch: as to make or bring frogs real or seeming, and other things at the Magicians of *Egypts* endeavour, and to bring up Gods *Elohim*, *i. e* Spirits invisible, likeness or shapes out of the earth at the call of the Witch at *Endor*.

But some have denyed all such familiarity with the Devil, because say they, *The Devil being a Spirit there cannot be such commerce or intimacy between Men & Spirits, as amounts to a Covenant engagement between them?*

To which I answer, there may be a covenant engagement between Men & Spirits. For,

1. There may be a Covenant between God and man: All *Israel* was in Covenant with God, *Deut.* 29. 12, *&c. That thou shouldest enter into Covenant with the Lord thy God.* And all Gods people did make a Covenant with God by Sacrifice, *Psal.* 50.   And before *Moses* & *Aaron* wrought their Miracles before *Pharaoh*, they were not only in covenant with God, but God had especially covenanted with, or promised to them, that upon their doing as he commanded and directed them, these miraculous
effects

effects should follow, *Exod* 7. 10. *&c.* Why
then may not men be in covenant with Satan
who is but a finite Spirit ? And as an effect &
token of it come after the working of Satan,
with all power and signs and lying wonders,
2 Thes. 2. 9.

2. The Lord forbids his people making a
Covenant with the Heathen Gods, *Exod.* 23. 32.
Thou shalt make no covenant with them, nor with
their Gods, that is, with the Devils, *Deu.* 32. 17.
If there had been no danger of *Israel* making
such Covenants, they would not have had such
a prohibition.

3. Satan discoursing with the Man Christ
Jesus, *Math.* 4. 8, 9. Offers to make a bargain
or covenant with Him, wherein he promiseth,
Quid pro Quo. Satan offers on his part to give
all the kingdoms of the World, and the Glory of
them ; and the condition he proposeth on
Christs part, is, *That Christ shall fall down and*
worship him. Had our blessed Saviour agreed
to these propositions there had been a bargain ;
but that was not possible, for when the
Prince of this world came to our Saviour, he
found nothing in him ; that is, no matter for
his temptations to work upon, *Joh.* 14. 30. But
alas, how many wicked men and woman are
there in the world, that would accept of such
bargains ? Some have been so set upon obtaining their desired ends, that to have their Wills
they will do as he said in the Poet.

Flectere si nequeo superos Acheronta movebo.

If I cannot obtain my wish and will from God, I will to Hell to fetch it thence. And if persons are prepared for it, and Satan sees it his interest, he will offer conference with them, as he did with *Eve, Gen.* 3. And readily promise them all the world can afford them according to their hearts desire, to the uttermost of his power, and make no scruple of lying, and if mankind believes him, Satan profers some condition to be performed on mans part, as he did to Christ; *If thou wilt worship me.* And when mankind believes & accepts the seeming good desired and offered, upon performance of the conditions required, here's a Covenant explicit or implicit. But say some, what ever Satan is said to do or reveal by a Witch, cannot he do the same things without a Witch?

A. 1. Satan hath done great things without Witches, as in the afflicting *Job*, and the possessed, as abovesaid,

2. Yet Satan doth also do and discover things by magicians, &c. as in the cases of the *Egyptian* Sorcerers, and woman at *Endor,* above expressed. And this may proceed, (1) Partly from the righteous Judgment of God, giving Satan both permission and commission at such times, to do great things in punishment to those that seek unto him in that way. As when *Ahab* goes to the Prophets that were not the Prophets of *Jehovah* or the Lord, 1 *King.* 22. 7.

but

but of the Devil, to enquire, whether he shall go to *Ramoth Gilead* : The Lord gives the Devil a commission to deceive *Ahab*, who by going to these Prophets went to the Devil, 1 *King.* 22. 20, 21, 22, 23. *Who will perswade Ahab ? And a Spirit said, I will perswade him, ... I will be a lying Spirit in the mouth of his Prophets.* Now hear Satans commission : *Thou shalt perswade him and prevail also : go forth & do so.* (2) Satan may in pollicy do many things (the Lord permitting) at the devotion of his Votarys, which he will not do at other times if he could, because hereby he carrys on his design of destroying Souls ; both of his Votarys, and of them that go unto them. For there be many that have so much natural Conscience in them, and so much aversation from the Devil, and horror at his presence, that they will not seek immediately to the Devil, who yet will be drawn to seek unto Wizards, and such as have familiar Spirits, and so fall into the Snare of the Devil, to the ruine of their Souls.

We know Satan is called the God of this World, and by imitating the Lords methods in shewing mercy to man, he seemed to the Heathen to be like the Most High : As *Lucifer* said, *Isa.* 14. 12, 14. Had the Lord his Ark, Temple, &c. where to give answers to his people ? So Satan had his Temples and Oracles, and Priests, whereby to give answers to his Worshippers, as at *Ekron*, at *Delphos*, and

else

elsewhere ; see *Acts* 14. 13. Did the Lord require faith in them that came to him ? So Satan requires especial faith in them that seek to him for help. Doth the Lord hearken to the voice of a man in working wonders? *Josh.*10. 14. So Satan will hearken to the voice of his Magicians, *&c.* Doth the Lord require particular actions to be done by his Servants, when they work wonders in his Name ? As *Aaron* must cast down his rod at one time, smite the rock with it at another time, speak to the rock at another time. *Elijah* prays at one time on his face between his knees, at another time otherwise, 1 *King.* 18. 42. So Satan had his various ceremonies, words and actions to be observed by those that obtained special help from him. As Charmings, Mutterings, Peepings, speaking low, *&c. Isa.* 8. 19 *&* 29. 4. And divers Sacrifices made to him, whereby he was honoured by the Heathen as a God. *Deut.* 32. 17. And Satan being thus served by them, did also some things for them, and that not only in way of operation, as for the *Egyptian* Magicians ; but also to some he did reveal truly some future events ; as appeareth by the warning given, *Deut.* 13. 1, 2, 3. where it's shewed that a Prophet in the name, and by the help of a false God, may foretel a Sign that shall come to pass.

And doubtless *Belzebub* did it at *Ekron* sometimes foretel truly future events, or else *Ahaziah*
would

would not have sent to him to know whether
he should recover at that time or not. But
the essence of their being a Witch or Sorcerer,
did not consist in their obtaining the desired
assistance from their God ; but rather in their
putting themselves into that way of endeavou-
ring to get help of their Gods. For the Astrologers, &c of *Babylon* are called Sorcerers or
Witches. *Isa.* 47.12. Though by their Inchantments and Sorceries they could not profit
themselves. And the Prophets of *Edom*, and
other heathens, *Jer.* 27.3, 9. are called Sorcerers for prophecying by Satan, though they prophecyed falsely. And so I conceive the Four
hundred and fifty Prophets of *Baal*, did all
use Sorcery or Inchantments in their invocation of *Baal*, and using actions they esteemed
acceptable to him, that they might procure by
him fire from Heaven to consume their Sacrifice, although they could not obtain it. 1 *King.*
18. 12. to 30. And so justly deserved death by
the Law. *Exod.* 22.18. and by the Law. *Exod.*
22.22. For Sacrificing to a false God.

Thus we see who were the Witches among
the Heathen : We may then query, *Who were*
the Witches among the Israelites that were to be put
to death ?

A. 1. Those that having the knowledge of
the true God, or at least the means, whereby
they might know him, did so far forsake the
true God, as to sue unto, and depend upon the
Devil,

Devil, or another God, as the Heathen Priests and Prophets that were Sorcerers did. As by having a familiar spirit as the Witch at *Endor* had; or by using Witchcrafts as *Manasseb* did. These as Apostates from God, and Votaries of the Devil, were to dye by the Laws. *Exod.* 22. 18,20. As is said of *Baals* Prophets. And such if they prophecyed in the name of those false Gods (whether the Prophesie were true or false,) were to dye by the Law. *Deut.* 18. 20. The Prophet that shall presume to speak in the name of other Gods, that Prophet shall dye.

2. Those persons who did prophecy a falsehood in the name of the Lord; or prophecy in his name when he sent them not, are called Diviners, though they pretended to speak (not in the name of false Gods, but) in the name of the true God; as, *Jer.* 28. 8, 9. *Mich.* 3. 7. Though they are not indeed called Witches or Sorcerers, but Diviners, which note a crime near to the former. Because they were so like unto the Diviners of the Heathen in prophecying falsly; and were alike capital offenders by that Law. *Deut.* 18. 20, 22. The Prophet which shall presume to speak a word in my name, which I have not commanded him to speak, shall dye, &c. So that although they are not called Witches, but Diviners, yet they were to dye by the Law, as well as the other.

Here then we may observe, who is to be, esteemed a Capital Witch among Christians
viz.

viz. those that being brought up under the
means of the knowledge of the true God, yet
being in their right mind, or free use of their
reason, do knowingly & willingly depart from
the true God, so as to devote themselves unto,
and seek for their help from another God, or
the Devil, as did the Devils Priests, and Prophets of old that were Magicians.

The end of such devoting to another God
is for some supposed benefit.   As, 1. To get
help from him ; So *Ahaz* seems to be a Witch
or Sorcerer, in that he sacrificed to the Gods
of *Syria*, that he might obtain help by them,
2 *Chron.* 28. 3, 23. His burning his Children in
the fire, after the Heathen abomination, is also a sin reckoned with Witchcraft ; see, *Deutr.*
18. 11. He was if not a Witch in sacrificing
himself, yet at least one that did seek after
Wizards and the like, to Sacrifice for him.   •

2. Another end in seeking help, is thereby
to do strange things, as did the *Egyptian* Sorcerers as above-shewed. And such a Sorcerer the
beast, *Rev.* 13. 13,14 prophecyed of, seems to
be, for he maketh fire to come down from
Heaven, on the Earth in the sight of men.
And this was the work of Satan upon *Job's*
Sheep and Servants, *Job* 1. 16.

3. Another end is for the discovery of Secrets ; as above shewed, from *Deut.* 13, 1, 2,3.
& 1 *Sam* 28

4. Another end is to prevent or remove
some

some evil felt, or feared ; as the Sorcerers of *Babylon*, that by their Sorceries sought to prevent, or save them from the evils coming upon them. And though they did not obtain the help aimed at from their Gods, yet they are stiled Sorcerers, *Isa.* 47. 12, 13, 14. *&* 44 25.

2. I say, brought up under the means of the knowledge of the true God ; for though many Witches were among the Heathen Nations, yet they were not to be put to death, because they knew not the true God, they knew no better. But as for thee, saith God, *The Lord thy God hath not suffered thee so to do ; and there shall not be found among you an Enchanter, Witch,* &c. *Deut.* 18. 9, 10, 14. And therefore the Lord made this Law, as an hedge to keep his people from going away from him to Devils, *to Gods whom they knew not, and whom their fathers feared not, Deut.* 32. 16, 17. And so this Law hath some affinity with that capital Law, the next verse, *but one step, Exod* 22. 20. *He that Sacrificeth to any God, save unto Jehovah only, shall be put to death.* So that *Daniel* did well in seeking to save the *Babylonian* Wise men, though Witches, *Dan.* 2. 14 *&c.* For they fell not under the Law. *Exod.* 22. 18. But being ignorant of the true God, needed to live, and be instructed, that thereby they might be made sensible of their evil practices, and turn unto the living God.

3. The object sought unto is the Devil, or
another

I

another God. Some of the Heathen did not
seek to the Devil, as a Devil, that is, as a ma-
licious, wicked, and unclean spirit: but as to
their God whom they thought ought to be
Worshipped by them. And some of the *Israelites*
had an opinion of many Gods, as *Ahaz*, 2 *Chr.*
28. 23. *Manasseh* and *Amaziah*, *Chap* 25. 14.
& 33 3, 4, 6. And so sacrificed to the Heathen Gods, as well as to their own. And this
was very abominable to the Lord to be ranked
thus with Idols and Devils, *Isa.* 42. 8. *Jehovah*
will not give his Glory to another.

4. The person I say, that hath the free use
of their reason; hereby are exempted from the
guilt of this crime, persons possessed or obsessed of the Devil, who did by the power of
Satan, strange things, as breaking chains, and
Lunatick persons, upon whom the Devil took
advantage by reason of their Lunacy.

5. They devote themselves to Satan, or their
other God, and to seek to him; which was
done divers ways; as by enchantments, charmings, peepings, muttering, sacrificing, cutting
themselves, prayers, &c. And though of later
times Satan as a cunning Fisher changeth his
baits, yet still all that seek to him, as his peculiar Votaries, have their Ceremonies, Ordinances by which Satan is invocated and worshipped. Here we must distinguish between those
that go and seek to Satan immediately, and
those that seek to him by the mediation of a
Wizard,

Wizard, *&c.* as *Saul* by the Witch at *Endor.*
The former sort only are called Witches, or
dealers with familiar spirits : But the latter is a
great sin prohibited and condemned, *Lev.* 19.
31. *& 20. 6.* & elsewhere.

6. I say ; do knowingly and willingly seek,
&c. And here I excuse a *tanto,* though not a
toto, those that ignorantly use charms, spells,
writings or forms of words, *&c* being taught
them by others, which are a kind of Witchcraft ; but those that use them are not sensible,
that they are but various ceremonies to invocate
the Devil, and that the effects following these
charms, *&c.* are done by the Devil. So some
have pulled fish bones out of a wound, cured
tooth ach, agues, warts, and stopped blood by
such devillish means. Such have an implicit
faith that the means used, shall produce the
effect desired, but consider not how ; and so
are beguiled by the Serpent that lies in the
grass unseen.

I knew a man in the *East,* who professed the
art of curing wounds, and stenching blood by
a form of words. I discoursed him about it,
and he told me, he had been in the practice
of it ; and believed it to be the gift of healing
given him from God, upon the use of some
Scripture words he used, as he had been taught
by an Old woman, and had tried it upon himself ; having cut his leg almost half through
with an Adds, and only bound up the wound
with

with a cloth, and laid over the wound those
words, and without other means the wound
was cured in a few days. I desired to hear
the words, and he related them to me, and I
found him almost as ignorant in Scriptures, as
an Heathen, and found he could not read.
Whereupon I informed him that part of his
words were Scripture, and part not; and that
those words upon which the greatest stress
was laid in order to the cure, were a perverse
addition to the Scriptures a meer fiction of
mans invention, and declared to him, that if
any such healing followed upon such a form
of words, it could not come from the efficacy
of the words themselves, or from a divine
conenience working a wonder, because of
those words, which were indeed a lye in the
additions made; therefore if any vertue were
in them, it came by the Devil, and so those
words a kind of Sorcery. The man hereby
seemed convinced of his error, and promised
reformation. I do not believe this man was a
Wizard (though in danger of it) because he
did it ignorantly in misbelief.

I hear some young persons through a vain
curiosity to know their future condition, have
tampered with the Devils tools, so far that
hereby one door was opened to Satan to play
those pranks; Anno 1692. I knew one of the
Afflicted persons, who (as I was credibly informed) did try with an egg and a glass to
find

find her future Husbands Calling ; till there
came up a Coffin, that is, a Spectre in likenes
of a Coffin.   And she was afterward followed
with diabolical molestation to her death ; and
so dyed a single person   A just warning to o-
thers, to take heed of handling the Devils weapons, left they get a wound thereby.

Another, I was called to pray with, being under sore fits and vexations of Satan.   And upon
examination I found she had tryed the same
charm : and after her confession of it and manifestation of repentance for it, and our prayers
to God for her, she was speedily released from
those bonds of Satan.   This iniquity though I
take it not to be the Capital crime condemned,
Exod. 22. Becaue such persons act ignorantly,
not considering they hereby go to the Devil;
yet borders very much upon it : and is too like
Sauls going to the Witch at *Endor*, and *Ahaziah*
sending to the God of *Ekron* to enquire.

CHAPTER. XV.

I proceed now to speak of some kinds of
these Devilish artists, not by an exact distri-
bution of them into their several species.   For
though they are distinguished by several names
and practices, yet they all agree in the general
crime of Witchcraft, and being thereby as it
were the Devils Priests and Prophets, depend-
ing upon his aid and oracles ; so that he that is

of one kind may be also of another, or all the
rest, according to their several ends for which,
and ways by which they make their applicati-
ons to the Prince of darkness : and as he is
pleased to communicate of his skill or power to
the answering of their expectations for a re-
ward of their dependance upon him. And as
of old, they had several names, as Magicians, Diviners, &c. So of late times, they have their several names, and in part several kinds of skill, or
power, as Conjurers, Astrologers, Cunning men,
Mathematicians, Witches, &c. But all of them
if they have their knowledge, or skill, or working by the Devil, are in Satans black list of
Witches. Some such there have been who divine by representing a person, or coffin, or
thing sought after in a looking glass, to discover
to the person enquiring somewhat secret, or
future. I have heard several credible Stories
of such Conjurers ; and shall relate one here
that I suppose was never in Print. An ancient
Woman related to me, *That when she was a*
Maid, she had a curiosity to know who should be her
Husband, and was informed of a Doctor that would
shew Maids their future Husbands in a glass: To
him therefore she went with her Money in her hand,
so know who should be her Husband ; and he carry-
ed her to a great looking glass, where she saw a man
in his full proportion whom she never saw before:
And a while after met this man (represented in the
glass) in the street, and having on the same

Cloaths

Cloaths he was represented with from head to foot ; and soon after he came a Suitor to her, and she was Married to him, and was her Husband when she made this Relation.   In this relation observe,

1. It was no doubt a truth, for she told me this in way of craving my advice, whether she had done well or evil in going to the Dr. and I told her, she did evil in going thereby to the Devil. 2. It was no delusion of her phantasie, or affection working toward any person ; for it was one she never saw before, that was now shewed unto her. 3. The Dr. could not bring into the glass the shadow of a man absent and unknown, by any natural cause, or means by him used. Therefore it was from the Devil, who raised this Spectre in likeness of a man then unknown. 4. And the Dr. doing this frequently for his Money, must know he did it by a familiar Spirit, and therefore was a Conjurer in some league explicite, or implicite with Satan. And I have heard and read of other Stories of this kind very credible, which satisfy me, that this was not the only Conjurer in *England.* But it may be queried,

Q. *How could Satan foretel this woman who should be her Husband, it being then a future contingent thing ?*

A. In this case, it might be easy for Satan to give a very probable conjecture ; for the man was a *Newfoundlander* that came to *England* for a Wife, as directed by his friends unto his

I 4   young

young woman: And the Devil knew of his
coming, he being at that time upon the Sea
thitherwards, or newly come on ſhoar ; and
the Devil knew his errand, and the quality and
conditions of both parties (as he is a diſcerning,
peircing ſpirit ;) and ſo knew it very probable
to be a Match. And by this repreſentation in
the glaſs impoſeth upon her Superſtitious ignorance, a kind of belief of a neceſſity to accept
him when he came. But in other caſes, its
not ſo eaſy.

Q. Here then we may enquire, *How can the
Devil know things to come ? Is not this Gods prerogative ? Iſa* 41. 22, 23.

A. Its true that the Lord alone knows things
to come, ſo that neither man or Angel can
know future events, unleſs the Lord make them
known, or afford means whereby the creature
may attain to know them : *Shew us things to
come hereafter, that we may know that ye are Gods.
Of that day and hour knoweth no man, no not the
Angels of Heaven, Math.* 24. 30. *Rev.* 5. 3, 4.
*None in heaven, or earth, or under the earth, was
able to open the book (ſealed with ſeven ſeals)
and to looſe the ſeales thereof.* Many other Scriptures ſpeak of our ignorance of things & times
to come, *Prov.* 27. 1. *Eccl.* 8. 7. *&* 6. 12.

2. Yet God affordeth means whereby men,
who are far leſs diſcerning than Spirits, come
to know many futurities certainly, and of o-
thers probably to gueſs, ſo as generally or for
the

the moſt part it proves according to mans fore-ſight. *A wiſe man fore-ſeeth the evil, Prov. 22. 3. & 27. 12.*

1. By viſions and revelations and ſuch like, ſo God revealed to *Abraham* and *David*, the conditions of their Poſterity for a great while to come, 2 *Sam. 7. 19.*

2. The Prophecyes, promiſes & threatnings in Scripture are a ſtanding revelation of futurities, in matters religious, civil, political & natural, as the changes of ſeaſons, &c. *Gen 8. 22.*

3. Many things are fore-known by their cauſes. As that wood thrown into the fire will be burnt, &c. And thus many Phyſitians fore-ſee the death of a perſon ſick of an incurable diſeaſe, when neither they nor their relations are ſenſible of it.

4 Many things are fore known by the uſual ſignes that go before them, which though they are not proper cauſes of the effects following, yet are concurrent with them. *As when the Fig-trees branch is tender Summer is nigh, Math. 24. 32.* A red skie in the evening is a ſign of fair morning ; and a red skie in the morning lowring of foul weather, and ſo it comes to paſs, *Math. 16. 1, 2, 3. Luk. 12. 54, 55, 56.*

5. Some things men foreſee very probable to come to paſs, becauſe themſelves or others have intended and contrived how to bring them to paſs. As *Saul* fore tells to *Jabeſh-Gilead ; They ſhall have help to morrow by that time the Sun be hot,*

hot, 1 *Sam.* 11. 9. Becauſe he intended and contrived it.

6. By obſervation & experience of the uſual events of providence, in the way of Gods go. verning the world ; a wiſe man fore knows probably at leaſt, what will come to paſs under like circumſtances.   And among men, one fore·ſeeth things to come farther than another ; as he excels another in prudence.   As the prudent fore ſeeth, *when the ſimple paſs on, and are puniſhed, Prov. 22. 3. Or hath had a larger experience than another, Eccl. 8. 5. A wiſe mans heart diſcerneth time and judgment.*

1. In all the above mentioned ways, except the firſt, Satan hath the ſame advantage to know future events as man hath ; and many advantages above· man.   (1.) As he is more knowing, wiſe, and of a larger underſtanding than man.   (2.) In that as a Spirit, he pierces more into the inſides and ſecrets of perſons, actions and things.   He cannot know the heart of man immediately, that is Gods pre· rogative, *Jer.* 17. 10 Yet ſo far as the heart diſcovers it ſelf by its operations, upon the ſenſes, external and internal, and other members of the body, Satan will find it out.   (3.) By the ſwiftneſs and multitude of thoſe Legions of unclean Spirits ; they are preſent in all Companies, Counſils, Cabals, and affairs of the Children of men, even with the Sons of God when they worſhip God ; and with the

Sons

Sons of men in all the compaſs of the earth. *Job* 1. 6, 7. (4) They have their experiences of five thouſand years ſtanding. (5.) When they intend and contrive any deſign upon the children of men, they are not in danger of being prevented by death (as men often are) for Spirits cannot dye; and ſo more probably foretel the events of their own counſels.　And by all the means and advantages above-ſaid, Satan can fore-ſee future contingent events much farther off than man can, and ſo foretell (the Lord ſuffering) a ſign or wonder which ſhall after come to paſs.

2. Satan hath alſo the advantage of fore-knowing, and fore ſhewing future things by ſome way of divine revelation at ſome times, for the puniſhment of men.　So God by ſome means (the way whereby to us unknown) lets the Devil know the death of *Saul* and his Sons, and reveal it to *Saul* for his puniſhment in going to ſeek to Satan ; and ſo Satan knows the way to deſtroy *Abab*, and that from God ; and contrives a way to bring it about, *viz.* by being *a lying Spirit in the mouth of* Ahabs Pro- *phets.*

3. Yea, the Lord ſucceeds the diabolical divinations of the King of *Babylon*, to prophecy ſucceſs unto him againſt *Judab*, for the puniſhment of *Judabs* ſins. *Ezek.* 21. 18. *to* 25. From this place obſerve, (1.) That the King of *Babylon* intending War againſt *Rabbath* and *Jeruſalem,*

Jerusalem, knew not which to go first unto.
(2.) Therefore he useth divination by arrows,
by consulting an Image or *Teraphim,* and by
looking into the liver of some beasts (always
used by the heathen) so that if the divination
favour the right hand, he will go first to *Jerusalem* : If the left, to *Rabbah.* (3.) These
divinations had no natural power in them to
direct them, but they were means whereby
they enquire of their Gods, that is the Devil.
(4) The Lord so over-rules the divination,
that is the Devils Oracle by the Image, *&c.*
that the answer shall be, *Go to Jerusalem and
prosper;* and accordingly he goes and prospers.
(5.) The Lord grants such success (not ap-
pointing the sin) unto these devillish divinations for the punishment of his apostate people.
But when ever the Lord pleaseth, he disap-
points all the Devils Ordinances. So that the
Devil cannot know, or cannot discover to his
Vassals what shall come to pass. *Isa.* 44. 25. *He
frustrateth the tokens of the lyars, and maketh diviners mad, and maketh their knowledge foolish.*

1. Then Inchantments, Sorceries, Astrologers, *&c.* shall not be able to save from evil,
or to profit, *Isa.* 47. 12, 13, 14.

4. If all the ways above-said so fail the Devil, that he cannot foretel what shall be hereafter, he hath an art by the ambiguity of his answers, to salve his credit, be the event which
way it will. So 1 *King.* 22. 6. He tells *Ahab;*
The

The Lord shall deliver it into the hand of the
King ; but doth not determine which King,
whether of *Syria*, or *Israel*. So in his Oracles
of old to *Cresus*. *Cresus Halyn penetrans mag-*
nam disperdet opum vim. Like the Sophism u-
sed against King *Edward* the Second. To
shed King *Edwards* Blood refuse to fear, I
count it good. And this shall suffice to speak
of this kind of Divining.

 2. Another sort of Diviners are they that
reveal secrets, as where Stollen Goods are hid,
or how Persons and Vessels do at Sea, or in
other Countries, which they pretend to know
by the Stars, and Positions of the Heavens;
but indeed by a familiar spirit. These are by
way of distinction called, Astrologers, Mathematicians, &c. Such, *Isai* 47. 13 are called,
Hiberei Shamajim, Observers of the Heavens,
(translated Astrologers) And *Hachotsim Be-*
shochabim, Beholders of the Stars, or Star gaz-
ers. But whatever men pretend, the Stars
cannot reveal such secrets.

 1. Suppose two men go to Sea in the same
Ship, from *England* to *Barbadoes*, and one dy-
eth, and another liveth ; they go out, continue
at Sea, and come to the Island both of them
under the same position of the Stars. How
then can the Heavenly Bodies tell the Astrologer in *England*, that one man is dead, and the
other alive ? So *Perkin* and *Paules* - steal each
an Horse out of the same Stable, at the same
time;

time ; *Perkin* carries his stollen Horse to *Bri-stol*, and *Paulet* carries his to *Exeter*, both at one time ; how can the Stars direct the Mathematician to find one Horse at *Exeter*, and the other in *Bristol*? they cannot, but the Devil can.

2. The Stars have their regular motion continued the same, according to the Law God laid upon them at first, *Psa.* 19. 4, 5, 6. & 104. 19. The fixed Stars continue in their orb, and the planets in theirs, whether men steal or be honest, go abroad or stay at home, are sick or well. *They are for signs and seasons* ; but not to point out the arbitrary actions of or contingent events upon men. Mr. *Lee*, the late learned Minister of the Gospel in *New Bristol*, related a credible Story of a Gentleman in *Hartford-shire*, ' Who had studied the Rules of Astrology, and ' being much urged, tryed by them to find ' for his friend a stolen Horse; but when ' by all the rules of his art, he could find no-' thing, sat musing with his eyes shut, and just ' such a Horse as the man described, was re-' presented to his Imagination, going with two ' men into a Stable, at such an Inn, in such a ' Town : He directs the man to go thither : ' he did so, and found his Horse, and returned ' to thank the artist. The Astrologer told him, ' it was the Devil suggested it to his Imagina-' tion, and thereupon resolved never more to ' meddle with that art,

3. The

3. The insufficiency of these rules of them-selves appear, in that those that seek for help by these artists, must have a belief, that they can help them, or else they cannot discover any thing to them. But if it were by pure art, the rules would be as effectual when people come without such a faith, as with it. ' I
' knew a very pious Matron, who when she was
' young in *England*, had lost some goods, and in
' her ignorance, went to a cunning man to
' find them. He told her he could not help
' her, unless she did believe he could. She
' answered, she believed in God, (or hoped in
' God) he could. Nay replied he, if you be-
' lieve in God, I cannot help you. And so she
' returned without her goods, but with a con-
' viction that she had gone to the Devil for
' help, and was not aware of it. Another relation like this, Mr. *Sherman* of *Boston* told me
concerning himself. ' He being in *England*
' was unawares brought into the Company of
' such a Mathematician, to whom diverse came
' and gave him Money, to tell them, how, and
' where their friends & vessels were, that went
' over sea. And he after he had raised his
' Scheams, and made his calculations, gave them
' such informations as they were satisfyed in.
' And at length, understanding Mr. *Sherman*
' was a *New England* man, asked, if he would
' know the state of his friends in *New England*.
' *Sherman* replyed, there were none of his Art
'   ' in

' in *New-England* : (Oh that it may be always
' so said of us !) but he had heard of this pro-
' session : it was said, they could inform none
' that did not believe they could help them :
' And he did not believe. The Artist reply-
' ed, he did it by pure Art, and would have
' *Sherman* try him, which at last he did. Tell
' me, said he, where my Father and Mother
' now are, and how they do. The Astrolo-
' ger asked him many questions, and after he
' had tryed the rules of his Art, said ; They
' were both alive in good health in *Boston* in
' *New England*. This is not so, said *Sherman*,
' for they were both dead before I came
' thence ; and I told you, that you could not
' help me unless I did believe.

These two Relations agree with what Mr.
Perkins urgeth against Judicial Astrologers.
Chap. 3. *p.* 80 *Viz.* That they *cannot help those
that come doubting* of their ability, or in a way
to tempt the Astrologer.

3. A third sort of these Diviners are such as
pretend to tell persons their Fortunes (as they
call it) or future Condition by looking into
their Hands. I have been acquainted with
some who have acquainted me with strange
futurities, these Fortune tellers have informed
them of, which after came to pass ; such as
man could not foretel but by the Devil, no nor
the Devil, but by some Judicial Act of God
over-ruling their Predictions, as he did the
divinations

divinations of *Nebuchadnezzar. Ezek.* 21. 21. above-mentioned. The vanity and falshood of the pretended Art of *Chyromancy* to predict by, appeareth. (1) In that there is no such variety of strokes or marks in the hands or faces of men and women, as there be variety of conditions in mans life which they pretend to find out by these marks. (2) If there were any such predicting Characters stamped by nature upon the bodies of persons; these Fortune-tellers are the most unlikely to know them; they being generally illiterate, ignorant of nature, art, religion, reason, history, & experience, and scarce a degree above bruit beasts.

Let all be warned then of the great sin and snare that is in hearkening to such Soothsayers; the scope of their profession being to draw men off from dependance upon God, and his guiding Providence in obedience to his Scripture Commands, with faith resting upon his promises, to lean upon the predictions of Fortune-tellers, who whether they prophecy good or evil, ensnare those exceedingly that enquire of them: for if they prophecy good, they are eagerly lifted up with doubtful expectation of its accomplishment. If it be evil, they are hanging upon a wrack of doubtful fears and terrors, which rob them of the comfort of their times of health and prosperity, contrary to the advice given them, *Eccl.* 2. 24 & 3. 12, 22. These above-named use Witchcraft in way of divination.

K   4. There

4. There be a fourth sort, whose exercise is more in operation, *viz.* such as cast a mist before the eyes of others by their Witchcrafts, who are alluded unto, *Gal.* 3. 1. by the Greek word *Bascaino quasi phaesi Kaino.* They have their eyes so held or darkened, that they cannot see things as they are: So the false teachers did bemist the eyes of the *Galatians*, *viz.* the eyes of their minds, that they could not see Christ Crucifyed before their eyes. Alike unto these are they who raise the Devil, or Spectres in divers forms, doing strange things thereby. Of this sort was Dr. *Lamb* the notorious Conjurer, kil'd by the Mobile in *London*, in *Charles* the first his Reign. Mr. *Baxter* of Spirits, *Chap.* 7. p. 155, 156. Relates a well attested Story of Dr. *Lamb*, his raising in the middle of a room, a Tree, little fellows, apes, baskets, &c. all which soon vanished. I refer the Reader to Mr. *Baxter*, for the Story at large.

5. Another sort are such as they call white Witches; that by spells, charms, &c. will cure Diseases, and that more easily than men can, and fetch fish bones out of mens hands, &c. (1.) Note here that the Devil hath more skill in the knowledge of all healing medicines than any man: and more ability and dexterity to convey them insensibly unto any sore, than any mortal creature. (2.) That some have such an ambition to excel in Physick, & curing variety of wounds and diseases, that they will rather
ther

ther go to the Devil, then fail of their defired skill and honour thereby. Many credible Hiftories I have heard of this kind; but I fpare to enlarge in thefe things which have been fo fully handled by *Perkins*, and others.

CHAPTER. XVI.

I come now to fpeak concerning thofe that are called *Black Witches*, or *Malefick Witches*, who by their enchantments do call in the Devils aid, for revenge, to do hurt to the bodies, and health of their neighbours, or to their cattle, goods, and the like. Thefe are the perfons commonly called Witches, and againft whom the fpirits of men and the laws of men are moft bent, for their profecution and punifhment. Now that I have concerning fuch to fay, I fhall comprehend in the enfuing *Propofitions*.

Prop. 1. There have been many evils that have befallen man and beaft, which have been ungroundedly afcribed to Witchcraft, and fo to Witches, which proceed from other caufes: As from natural operations tho' hidden from thofe that fo fufpect or from the hand of God immediately, or from the hand of Satan without the concurrence of man kind; as hath been in part fhewed already in this enquiry above. Should an herd of Swine run violently down a fteep place into the Sea in thefe days and perifh in the waters, as did the *Gergefens* Swine,

K 2 *Matb.*

Matb. 8. 32. People would conclude they perished by Witchcraft ; and yet there was no such cause of the destruction.

Prop. 2. Melancholly and Imagination hath fancied many things to proceed from **Witches,** when there is no ground for it.

Prop. 3. Many impossible things for Witches, or the Devil to do by them, are related to be done by Witches : As the transmutation of bodies from men to beasts, *&c.* The going in Spirit to places far distant, and leaving their bodies behind ; as if the Devil could separate the Soul from the body, and restore it again at pleasure, which is to ascribe to him a divine power to restore the dead. Such things are either devised fictions, or abuses of the imaginations of them that so say of themselves : they, being only laid in a trance or dream, and so conceiting a change in them that never was. So some have affirmed they have been carryed many hundred miles through the air, to remote places, and brought back again in an hour or two, which cannot be without a miracle ; for so swift a motion through the air, would take away the breath of a person so transported, without an almighty power to sustain them.

Prop. 4. It must be granted that there is no clear instance of any such *Malefick* or *Black* Witch in Scriptures. The Magicians of *Egypt* or *Babylon,* or those mentioned *Act.* 8. 9, 10, 11. *&* 13. 8, 9, 10. *Jer.* 27. 9. *Isa.* 47. *Dan.* 2. *&* 4. *&* 5.

4. *& 5. chap.* are not charged with any such
crimes. The only instance I remember given
of such an one in Scripture is *Balaam* : but he
cannot be proved to be such an one. (1) Its
pleaded that *Balak* sent to him to come ; *For I
wot* (saith he) *that he whom thou cursest is cursed.*
And this indeed shews what an opinion *Balak*
had of him, *Numb* 22. 6. But when *Balaam*
answers the messengers, he tells them ; *As the
Lord,* i. e. Jehovah, *shall speak to me, I will bring
you word* : And Jehovah refuseth to give me
leave : *And the word that God putteth in my mouth,
that shall I speak.* v 8, 13, 38. So that whatever opinions *Balaam* might have of plurality of
Gods, yet he owns he could not curse *Israel* but
by the true God. See *Numb* 23. 1, 3 *with
Deut.* 23. 4, 5. *Josh.* 24. 9, 10. The Scripture
shews that *Balaam* sought not to curse *Israel,* but
by the everliving God. (2) And if it be said,
that *Balaam* saying, *There is no inchantment a-
gainst Jacob, neither divination against Israel, Cap.*
23. 23. Intimateth, That there may be inchantment and divination also against other people. ;
yet it doth not signify that *Balaam* used to curse
any without the assistance of the true God.
For he saith, *v.* 8. *How shall I curse whom God
hath not curse ? or how shall I defy, whom the Lord
hath not defied ?* He speaks as a man convinced,
that the power of all false Gods was unable to
bring a curse without Gods leave. *And if Balak would give him an house full of Silver & Gold,*

he

he faith, *he cannot go beyond the word of the Lord,*
or Jehovah, my God, *to do less or more.* Where
note, that *Balaam* openly professeth to these
heathen, that Jehovah is his God, and him he
will obey, *Numb.* 22. 18. And when the Angel
of Jehovah opposeth him, he submits so far
to him as to offer, if it displeased him, he
would go back again. And when he comes to
sacrificing, still it is to *Jehovah.* For he said,
Chap 23. 3. after he had offered, Peradventure
Jehovah will come & meet me, *&c.* and where
God met him, *He said unto him,* i. e. to Jehovah.
I have offered upon every altar a bullock & a ram,
and this was repeated again, and still *Balaam*
went to meet Jehovah, and Jehovah met him
once and again, and put a word in his mouth.
And *Balaam* spake the word Jehovah put into
his mouth: and when *Balaam* saw it pleased
Jehovah to bless *Israel, Chap.* 24. 1. All the circumstances of the place shew that all his address-
es were unto the living God, that by him he
might procure such a curse upon *Israel,* which
might do more against *Israel* then all the armies
of *Balak* could do.

Q *Why then is* Balaam *called a Soothsayer or Diviner, and said to use Inchantments ? and what are
those Enchantments? and why so called?*

A. These inchantments were the Sacrifices
mentioned, *Chap* 24. which were offered to the
true God For its said, *He went not as at other
times to seek for Enchantments :* This plainly re-
fers

fers to the times when he facrificed as above-
faid. *Heb.Chepagnam,bepagnam, i. e.* not this time
as the former time; namely the times when he
facrificed.   Thus *Ainfworth in locum*; all his former altars and facrifices were by the art of inchantment, or obferving fortunes.   But how
thefe were inchantments, feeing they were not
as the heathen inchantments to a falfe God, &
that facrificing was an Ordinance of God, is a
difficulty to underftand.   But I conceive they
are fo called, becaufe *Balaam* did pervert the
end and ufe of Gods Ordinance, and therein
imitate the Heathen.For God had faid to him,
Thou fhalt not curfe the people for they are bleffed Yet
Balaam by thefe Sacrifices will try to curfe them.
So heathen nations are faid to do, before they
warred againft any people to endeavour by
prayers, facrifices and enchantments to turn the
favour of God from them. Before the Heathen *Romans* Befieged any City, their Priefts,
called out the God, under whofe tutelage the
City was, that he would forfake the people,
Temples and holy things, and be Provoft unto
them, and accept of their City, *&c.* vowing to
him, if he would fo do, to honour him with
Temples, *&c.* And then offered Sacrifices to the
Dictator or Emperour, devoted, or curfed the
Enemies Cities and Armies, that they might be
filled with fear, terror, *&c. Balaam* acts his like.
Thefe and like the Charmers, *Maimony* fpeaks
of, who whifper over a wound, or read a verfe

K 4   out

out of the Bible: likewise he that readeth over
an infant, that it may not be frighted; or that
layeth the Bible, or the Phylacteries upon a
child that it may sleep: Such saith he, are In-
chanters or Charmers, because they make the
words of the Scripture, medicine for the body,
whereas they are not, but medicine for the
Soul. So *Balaam* makes a charm of an Ordinance of God: For neither *Balak* nor *Balaam* aimed to give honour & glory to God thereby,
but to use them as it were a bribe, to try if
thereby they could prevail with the Lord to
reverse his word, whereby he had said of *Israel*, *They are blessed*. For when he sees he cannot prevail, he saith, *God is not a man that he
should ly; and he hath blessed, and I cannot reverse
it*. Again, what *Balaam* did herein, it was not
sincerely for God, but for his hire, *Neh. 13. 2.*
Even for rewards of Divination, *Numb. 22. 7.*
For the wages of unrighteousness, 2 *Pet.* 2. 15. Pos-
sibly also there might be somewhat like inchantment in the manner of his sacrificing; as *Sacrificing in the high places* of Baal, *and on the top of
Peor*, places formerly dedicated to *Baal-Peor*.
Thus *Balaam* by his Enchantments deserved
the title of a Soothsayer or Diviner and mad
Prophet.

Prop. 5. Though there be no plain example
of a *Malifick* Witch; yet from what the Scripture saith of the power of Satan and his malice
against man, & of the wickedness that is in the
heart

heart of man ; we may see there is a possibility of such abominable creatures to be found in
the black list of Satans guard.   For,

1. Satan hath power when the Lord permits
him, to do mischief to the bodies and estates of
mankind, as already proved in the instances of
Job and others.

2. There be some persons so wicked that *A-
baz* like, they will sacrifice to and serve the
Devil, that he may help them.   And if in other
things, why not in revenging them upon those
they hate, as well as in other matters ? As *Israel*
slew their brethren in a rage that reached up
to heaven : so some will pursue their adversaries with a rage reaching down to hell.   And
excess of anger gives great advantage to the
Devil, *Eph.* 4. 26, 27. *Let not the Sun go down
upon your wrath ; neither give place to the Devil.*
If sinful anger gives the Devil a place, how
much more such a rage as whereby men go to
hell for aid against their foes ?   When men
seek to Satan for revenge, he will be ready to
further them in it ; by discoursing with them,
(as he did with *Eve*, yea with Christ himself,
Math. 4.) to see what he may gain upon them
thereby : or by tempting them to sacrifice to
him, or use his ceremonies and ordinances,
whereby, Satan is implicitely at least invoked
for to do his utmost on their behalf.   And Satan that promised to the spotless Lamb of God,
all the kingdoms of the world, will be ready

to promise such miscreants to revenge them on their adversaries, or any mischief they desire, if they will serve him. And at some times to perform his promise if the Lord suffer him, as the roaring Lyon that seeks to devour: or at least will pretend himself author, of the harms the envyed person sustaines. But if he cannot, yet he can answer such deluded creatures, that either they did not observe his direction, or that God hath set an hedge about the party maligned, or the like, and so keep up his credit still.

Mrs. *Got*, a very credible and pious woman, told me, *That her father Mr.* Palmer *lived nigh a man that acknowledged himself to be a Conjurer. On a certain day there came a violent wind upon Mr.* Palmers *house, as if it would blow it down: but it only blew down an Elm tree that stood in his Court yard. In process of time this Conjurer came to Mr.* Palmer *and confessed, that he had a grudge against him, and thereupon did invocate the Devil to do* Palmer *a mischief, and he promised to blow down* Palmers *house; but only blew down the Elm: whereupon the Conjurer taxed the Dæmon with breach of promise: But he answered* Palmer *was a Praying man, and God had set an hedge about all that he had need of, and so he had no power over his house; but the Elm being only for shew and recreation, he had power over that.*

As for matters of fact, I must refer to histories that speak of *Malefick* Witchcraft, wherein though many things are certain or fabulous,

there

there may be truth in some of those relations.
And by the above-mentioned, and other such
histories, we meet with of that kind, we may
gather, That when persons will seek to the Devil for revenge, he will either do harm to those
they hate, or if the Lord inflict by his hand upon
such persons hated by the Conjurers, Satan will
perswade the Conjurer, that he effected it in
persuance of their quarrel. But if the desired mischief be not effected, the Devil will have a plea
to excuse himself. But however they which by
themselves immediately invocate the Devil to
help them, to avenge themselves on those they
hate, are hereby *Malefick* Witches, whether
they obtain his help or not.

CHAPTER XVII.

HAving said thus much to shew what the
Witches condemned by Scripture are, I
shall reflect upon some assertions laid down in
a Book dispersed about *Salem, Anno 1695.* En-
tituled, *Truth held forth &c.* Published, by
Thomas Maul, pag. 221. He saith, What is the Devil, or Hell but nothing ? that God never created them, for they were *Non Entity,* a not being, which is contrary and perfectly opposite
to Entity and Being: And this might be the
Devil that dwelt in *Adam* which seduced him,
Pag. 185. He insinuates, That if people keep
Gods Commands, or are righteous persons, they
cannot

cannot be possessed or bewitched by the Devil or his Instruments; for the cause of their being possessed, or bewitched, hath been through a life of disobedience to God, *Pag* 190. Saith, The way to know one that is a Witch from one that is not a Witch, is by that wisdom, by which the Damosel, *Acts* 16. 16. was known to be a Witch. Unto these assertions, I answer, (1.) By the said *Thomas Maul* & his Wife : For when *B. B.* was upon her Tryal, the said *Mauls* Wife came in and testified against the said *B.B.* to prove her a Witch, in order to her Condemnation for Witchcraft: And the same day said *B.* was Executed, *T. Maul* said in my hearing, that if he had been desired to pray with her at her Execution, he would not; for he believed she was guilty of that sin the Scripture saith, we must not pray for it ; for he believed she was a Witch, and had covenanted with the Devil, & forsaken God ; and that was the sin we ought not to pray for. He said also that he could have come in a witness against her, if he would ; & that he believed she had bewitched to death a Child of his. And he believed most of those in Prison were Witches. From hence I gather, that in the year 1692. *T. Maul* did believe the Devil to be an Entity, & that a Witch by him had power to bewitch to death the Child of him that he esteemed a righteous person ; believing as others did, save that he counted a Witch guilty of the unpardonable sin. But when

others

others find an error in proceeding too far in these matters, he comes to see it also : And to avoid it, runs into another extream ; which I proye by the ensuing Propositions.

Prop. 1. The Devils were once holy Angels, created by God, and so Entities. This appeareth by many Scriptures before mentioned : As by his tempting our Saviour, *Mat* 4. Who had no corrupt quality within him; being the spotless Lamb of God ; yet him did Satan tempt, *yea take him up into the holy City, & set him on the pinacle of the Temple, and into an high mountain, and shew him all the Kingdoms of the World, and the glory of them.* These things could not be done by a *Non Ens.* I shall add some farther confirmation from other places, (1) *Jude* 6. Angels were created by God. The Devils are Angels. (2.) They that left their own habitation are Entities: But the Devils left their own habitation: Therefore Entities. (3.) They that sinned, and for their sin are delivered into *Chains of Darkness, to be reserved unto Judgment,* are Entities: But so did the Devil, 2 *Pet.* 2 4. Therefore, &c. (4.) He that is the Prince of this World, the *God of this World, the Prince of the power of the Air; he that goeth to and fro in the earth, and walketh up and down in it,* is a Being, an Entity. But such is the Devil, *Joh* 4. 7. *Job* 1 4, 30. 2 *Cor.* 4. 4. *Eph* 2.2. Therefore. So then the denying the Entity of the Devil, is a reviving the old Doctrine of the Sadduces, *Act.* 22. 8. Who said, *There is neither Angel nor Spirit.*   *Prop.*

Prop. 2. There was no Devil dwelt in *Adam* to seduce him before he was tempted by *Eve*, to *eat of the tree of knowledge of good and evil*. The Devil, saith he, is not a Being, yet dwelt in *Adam*, and seduced him: By this Devil in *Adam* then, he meaneth a sinful quality in *Adam* before he was tempted to eat, or it was a name without signification. But there could be no such evil quality in *Adam* before so tempted: For if it were, it must be created with him, or enter into him before *Eve* did tempt him: But neither of these, therefore not at all. Not the former, *for he was created upright*, Eccl 7. 29. *Very good, and in Gods Image*, Gen. 1. 26, 27, 31. Not the latter, for the Scripture gives no intimation of any evil in *Adam* before seduced by the woman (2) Nay the Devil that seduced him was without him, even the Serpent or Devil in the Serpent, that seduced *Eve* first by talking with her, and by her was he deceived, *Gen.* 3. 1. to 6. 2 Cor. 11. 3 1 Tim. 2. 14. *Adam was not deceived* (that is first) *but the woman*, &c. (3.) The Lord in punishing that first sin, doth distinctly punish *Adam*, *Eve* and the Serpent (in which is comprehended the Devil that old Serpent. *Gen.* 3. 14, 15. *with* 2 *Cor.* 11. 3. *Rev.* 20. 2.) as three distinct Entities or Beings; therefore the Devil was without, *ab extra*, before *Adam* was beguiled.

Prop. 3. All wicked men are not Witches; as *T. Maul* holds forth, p. 183. & 193. &c. Saying,

ing, *All that live a life of disobedience are Witches in some degree*, with more to that effect. For if all wicked persons were Witches in the sence intended, *Exod* 22 18. *Deut.* 18. 10. Then all wicked men should have been put to death by the law of *Moses*: But there was no such thing. Nay all the heathen Idolaters were not called Witches, or Sorcerers in *Egypt* or *Babylon*, but only some peculiar persons among them.   And if all had familiar Spirits, there had not been that need of such a warning, *Regard not them which have familiar Spirits, nor seek after Wizards, &c.*

Prop. 4. God hath no where promised all people that keep Gods Commands, or are righteous persons, that they shall not be possessed or bewitched by the Devil or his Instruments. Indeed it is sometimes so, as *Numb.* 23 21, 23 *There is no inchantment against Jacob, neither any divination against Israel; when God hath not beheld iniquity in Jacob, nor seen perverseness in Israel.* And our best shield against Satan, is faith in Christ, with prayer and an holy life.   Yet *Job* a perfect man did suffer more in his Body, Goods, Servants and Children then most wicked men in the World have done.   And it was a Daughter of *Abraham* whom Satan bound eighteen years, *Luk.* 13. 16. And a Mother of whom it is said, *O woman great is thy faith, be it unto thee even as thou wilt; who had a Daughter grievously vexed with a Devil possessing of her.* So that God in his Soveraignty makes all things come alike to all
when

when he pleaseth ; *so that no man knoweth love or hatred by any thing that is before him.*

Prop 5. The bewitching spoken of, *Gal.* 3.1. is not to be understood of a proper or literal bewitching, but in a Metaphorical sence, where by way of allusion, the false Teachers are compared to Witches, as being like them ; for as Witches have bewitched the eyes of the Body, so they bewitched the eyes of the mind. And though Witchcraft be one kind of the works of the flesh mentioned, *Gal* 5.19,20,21. Yet the Text doth not say, all the works of the Flesh are Witchcraft : But this is distinct from Murder, Drunkenness and the rest, as they are distinct each from other.

Prop. 6 The Wisdom of God doth no where say, that the Damosel mentioned, *Act.*16 16 was a Witch. But it describeth her to be a person possessed with a spirit of divination, or having a spirit of *Python* within her : Whom *Paul* in the name of Christ commanded to come out of her, and so he was cast out. That Spirit that calleth her a Witch, doth consequentially at least call the Damosel, *Mark* 7 25. a Witch, because she had an unclean spirit ; and so would render all the possessed in the Gospel, worthy of death by *Moses* Law ; which is to subvert all the Scriptures which condemn that abomination. It was therefore a blasphemous comparison which he made, who said, There was as great mistakes in the Scripture, as in *T. Mauls* Book ;

Book ; presuming therein to equalize to the
lively Oracles of God, a Book abounding with
gross mistakes in Doctrine and History.

Q. *How may a Witch, Sorcerer or Conjurer be
proved to be such as being legally convicted to receive the punishment appointed ? Exod* 27. 18.

A. I answer from 1 *Sam.* 28 *Chap.* We find
there *that Saul put away those that had familiar
Spirits, and Wizards out of the Land, verf.* 3. Yet
one was left at *Endor, v.*7. *Saul* then had a way
to convict them ; & the Woman at *Endor* points
at the way, *v.* 9. For *Saul* had said to her, *Divine unto me by the familiar spirit, and bring me
him up whom I shall name unto thee* : The Woman answers, *Wherefore then layest thou a snare for
my life, to cause me to dye ? q. d.* If it be proved
by sufficient witness, that I Divine by a familiar Spirit, and raise a Ghost from the Dead, I
must dy by the Law, But *Saul* sweareth to her
by the Lord, *As Jehovah liveth, there shall no
punishment happen to thee for this thing.* And then
she proceeds. Note, that this woman tho' she
dealt with and by the Devil, hath so much
knowledge of Jehovah, and confidence in an
Oath made by him, that she ventures her life
upon it. Again, *v.* 21. After she had raised the
supposed *Samuel,* she said unto *Saul* ; *I have o-
beyed thy voice, and have put my life in my hand.*
As if she had said, I have done that in obedience to thee ; that were it proved against me,
would take away my life. Here then we see

L   that

that if it can be proved against any, that they
have divined by a familiar spirit, or done such
like act of communion with the Devil, or raised the Dead by him that is the Devil in likeness
of the Dead; then such a person is proved to
be a Witch that ought to die: So in like manner, if any be proved to use Sorceries (as did
the Magicians of *Egypt*) among Christian people, such ought to dye, or proportionably by
familiarity with the Devil to do, or come to
know strange things, or work signs, lying wonders, or miracles by him, as they are called,
2 *Thes.* 2. 9 *Rev.* 13. 13, 14. *Deut.* 13. 1, 2.

Q. *But by what way may such Divinations and
Sorceries be proved ?*

A. In the same way that Murder, Theft,
and such like crimes are provable. As (1.) By
the testimony of two Witnesses, that the party
suspected hath used Sorcery, &c. (2.) Confession may in some cases be taken in this crime as
well as others, as hath been above-shewed; If
the persons be *compotes mentis*, and give as clear
demonstration of their guilt of the fact, as *Ba-
anah* and *Rechab* did of their slaying *Ishbosheth*,
when they brought his head to *David*, 2 *Sam.*
4. 6, &c. (3) The testimony of partners in the
crime in some cases, as above shewed, *Chap.* 11.
(4.) Circumstances antecedent to, concomitant
with, or suddenly consequent upon such acts of
Sorcery, have like force to fasten a suspicion of
this crime upon this or that person; as the like
circum-

circumstances have to fasten a suspicion upon any for another crime attended with them ; *mutatis mutandis.*

Here it may be enquired, *Whether persons obsessed, possessed, or under bodily torments or vexations by Satan, are fit witnesses?*

I answer in the ensuing Propositions.

Prop. 1. Those whose Bodies are sorely afflicted by the Devil, and yet their understandings clear and free, are fit to be Witnesses as well as others. As was *Job*, who when Satan had smitten him with sore boyls from head to foot, yet was a fit witness for God. *Job* 42. 7. *Speaking of God the thing that was right.*

Prop. 2. Some under these molestations of Satan have their understandings so darkened and phantasies so abused, that they are not in their right mind, till delivered from Satan, as was the case of the man among the Tombs, *Mark.* 5. 2, 3, 15. So the Damosel, *Acts* 16. 16, 17. Though she gave a true testimony concerning *Paul* and *Silas*, yet she was no fit witness, because she spake by the instigation of Satan, & not of her own knowledge. So it may be proportionably in persons under the influence of inchantment, or obsession by Satan, although in a lesser degree.

Prop. 3. Hence it may follow, that a person under these assaults of hell, may be fit for a witness at one time, when free from these fits, which darken his understanding: But not another

L 2   ther

ther time, *viz.* when the sences are beclouded
by the violence of their fits.   Again, they may
be fit to testifie to some things; namely to what
they feel and suffer upon their own Bodies: But
not of what they see at some distance, or about
external & remoter objects; because their eyes
& phantasies may be under some kind of fasci-
nation (as I may call it) of the Devil; so as to
mistake one thing for another.

Obj *But is it not then according to the principles*
laid down above, impossible to prove any person to
be a Witch, seeing the workings between Satan and
them are so secret? How can they be discovered?

A. Other Malefactors work secretly & in the
dark, hoping never to be discovered. *Job* 24. 14,
15, 16, 17 The Murderer, Thief, Adulterer, say,
no eye shall see me, & disguise their faces, dig
in the dark, *&c.* But the Lord searcheth out
such Malefactors, when settled on their lees,
with his candle of judgment, though they dig
deep to hide themselves from men; yea, & if
it were possible, from God himself. They say,
Who seeth us? who knoweth us, Zeph. 1 12. *Isa* 29.
15, 16. Yet the Lord brings all to light before
men when he pleaseth. So the Lord can & doth
discover Sorcerers, Magicians, and all sorts of
Witches, when, and as oft as he pleaseth; and
sometimes leaves them to discover and betray
themselves: And sometimes over-rules their
Master whom they serve, to intrap & deceive
them. Pro. 26. 26. *Whose hatred is covered by deceit,*
                                                                    his

*bis wickedness shall be shewed before the whole Con-
gregation.* Which is to be underftood when the
Lord pleafeth to bring to light thefe hidden
works of darknefs.

CHAPTER XVIII.

I Shall conclude this Difcourfe with fome
Application of the whole.

1. We may hence fee ground to fear, that
there hath been a great deal of innocent blood
fhed in the Chriftian World, by proceeding upon unfafe principles, in condemning perfons for
Malefick Witchcraft.

2. That there have been great finful neglects
in fparing others, who by their divinings about
things future, or difcovering things fecret, as
ftollen Goods, &c. or by their informing of
perfons and things abfent at a great diftance,
have implored the affiftance of a familiar fpirit,
yet coloured over with fpecious pretences, and
have drawn people to enquire of them: A fin
frequently forbidden in Scripture, as *Lev.* 19 31
& 20. 6. *Ifa.* 8. 19, 20. and yet let alone, and in
many parts of the World, have been counte-
nanced in their diabolical skill and profeffion;
becaufe they ferve the intereft of thofe that
have a vain curiofity, to pry into things God
hath forbidden, and concealed from difcovery
by lawful means. And of others that by their
incbantments, have raifed mifts, ftrange fights,

and the like, to beget admiration, and please Spectators, &c. When as these divinations and operations are the Witchcraft more condemned in Scripture than the other.

3. But to come nigher home, we have cause to be humbled for the mistakes & errors which have been in these Colonies, in their Proceedings against persons for this crime, above fourty years ago and downwards, upon insufficient presumptions and presidents of our Nation, whence they came. I do not say, that all those were innocent, that suffered in those times upon this account. But that such grounds were then laid down to proceed upon, which were too slender to evidence the crime they were brought to prove; and thereby a foundation laid to lead into error those that came after. May we not say in this matter, as it is, *Psal. 106. 6. We have sinned with our fathers?* And as, *Lam. 5. 7. Our fathers have sinned and are not, and we have born their iniquities?* And whether this be not one of the sins the Lord hath been many years contending with us for, is worthy our serious enquiry. If the Lord punished *Israel* with famine three years for a sin of misguided zeal fourty years before that, committed by the breach of a Covenant made four hundred years before that: 2 *Sam.* 21. 1, 2. Why may not the Lord visit upon us the misguided zeal of our Predecessors about Witchcraft above fourty years ago, even when that Generation is gathered to their Fathers.

4. But I would come yet nearer to our own times, and bewail the errors and miftakes that have been in the year 1692. In the apprehending too many we may believe were innocent, and executing of fome, I fear, not to have been condemned; by following fuch traditions of our fathers, maxime of the Common Law, & Prefidents and Principles, which now we may fee weighed in the balance of the Sanctuary, are found too light. I heartily concur with that direction for our publick prayers, emitted *December* 17. 1696. by our General Affembly, in an order for a general *Faft, viz. That God would fhew us what we know not, and help us wherein we have done amifs, to do fo no more : And efpecially that whatever miftakes on either hand, have been fallen into, either by the body of this people, or any order of men, referring to the late tragedy raifed among us by Satan and his Inftruments, through the awful Judgment of God: He would humble us therefore, and pardon all the errors of his Servants & People, that defire to love his Name, and be attoned to his land.* I am abundantly fatisfyed that thofe who were moft concerned to act and judge in thofe matters, did not willingly depart from the rules of righteoufnefs. But fuch was the darknefs of that day, the tortures and lamentations of the afflicted, and the power of former prefidents, that we walked in the clouds, and could not fee our way. And we have moft caufe to be humbled for error on

L 4

that

that hand, which cannot be retrieved. So that we must beseech the Lord, that if any innocent blood hath been shed, in the hour of temptation, the Lord will not lay it to our charge, but be merciful to his people whom he hath redeemed, *Deut.* 21. 8. And that in the day when he shall visit, he will not visit this sin upon our land, but blot it out, and wash it away with the blood of Jesus Christ.

5. I would humbly propose whether it be not expedient, that some what more should be publickly done then yet hath, for clearing the good name and reputation of some that have suffered upon this account, against whom the evidence of their guilt was more slender, and the grounds for charity for them more convincing. And this (in order to our obtaining from the Lord farther reconciliation to our land,)& that none of their surviving relations, may suffer reproach upon that account. I have both read and heard of several in *England,* that have been executed for Capital crimes, and afterwards upon sence of an error in the process against them, have been restored in blood and honour by some publick act. My Lord *Cook* relates a story. *A man going to correct a Girle his Neice, for some offence, in an upper room, the Girle strove to save her self, till her nose bled, and wiping it with a cloath, threw the bloody cloath out at the window, and cryed Murder; and then ran down staires, got away and hid her self. Her Uncle was prosecuted*

by

by her friends upon *suspicion* of *Murdering* her, because she could not be found. He declared that she
made her escape, as above said. Then time was allowed him to bring her forth, but he could not hear of
her within the time, and fearing he should dy if she
could not be found, procures another Girle very like
her, to appear in Court, and declare she was his
Neice that had been missing : But her relations examine this counterfeit, until they find her out, and she
confesseth she was suborned and counterfeited the true
Neice. Upon these presumptions the man was found
guilty of Murdering his Neice, and thereupon executed. And after his execution his true Neice comes
abroad & shews her self alive and well. Then all
that saw it were convinced of the Uncles innocency,
and vanity of such presumptions. The Printing &
Publishing of this relation Vindicates the good
name of the Uncle, from the imputation of the
crime of Murder. And this is one end of this
present discourse, to take off (so far as a discourse of this nature can) infamy from the
names and memory of such sufferers in this
kind, as do not deserve the same.

 6. Here it may be suitable for us to enquire,
What the Lord speaks to us by such a stupendous pro-
vidence, in his letting loose Satan upon us in this un-
usual way? *Ans.* 1. We may say of this, as our
Saviour said of his washing his disciples feet,
Joh. 13. *What I do thou knowest not now, but thou*
shalt know hereafter. The *Judgments of the Lord*
are a great deep, Psal. 36. 6. *How unsearchable are*

his judgments, and his ways past finding out?
2. Yet somewhat of his counsel at present for
our instruction may be known, by comparing
the Word and works of God together.

   1. As when *Joshua* the high Priest though an
holy chosen man of God, stood before the Angel, *Satan stood at his right hand to resist him,*
or to be his adversary : And the advantage Satan had was by the filthy garments *Joshua* was
clothed with before the Angels : That is, some
iniquity which yet was not passed away, *Zech.*
3. 1, 3, 4. So we may say here were among Gods
own Children filthy garments. The sins of Luke-
warmness, loss of our first love, unprofitableness
under the Gospel, slumbering & sleeping in the
wise, as well as foolish Virgins, worldliness, pride,
carnal security, and many other sins. By these
and such like sins the accuser of the Brethren
got advantage to stand at our right hand (the
place of an Accuser at Courts of Justice) and
there accuse us and resist us.

   2. When the *Egyptians* refused to let *Israel*
go to sacrifice and keep a feast to the Lord in
the Wilderness : *The Lord cast upon the fierceness*
of his wrath, by sending Evil Angels among them,
Psal. 78. 49. Egypts sins were (1.) Coveteous-
ness, they would not let *Israel* go, because they
gained by their labours. (2.) Contempt of God
and his Instituted Worship, and Ordinances.
They did not count them of such concernment, that *Israel* should go into the Wilderness

to obferve them. Both thefe fins have too much
increafed in our Land. (1.) Coveteoufnefs, an
inordinate love of the World gave Satan advantage upon us. (2.) Contempt of Gods Worfhip and Inftituted Ordinances. The Errand
of our Fathers into this Wildernefs, was to Sacrifice to the Lord ; that is, to worfhip God
in purity of heart and life, and to wait upon
the Lord, walking in the faith and order of
the Gofpel in Church fellowfhip; that they
might enjoy Chrift in all his Ordinances. But
thefe things have been greatly neglected and
defpifed by many born, or bred up in the
Land. We have much forgotten what our Fathers came into the Wildernefs to fee. The
fealing Ordinances of the Covenant of Grace
in Church-Communion have been much flight-
ed and neglected; and the fury of this Storm
raifed by Satan hath fallen very heavily upon
many that lived under thefe neglects. The
Lord fends Evil Angels to awaken and punifh
our negligence: And to my knowledge fome
have been hereby excited to enter into the
Chamber of Gods Ordinances, to hide themfelves, until the indignation be over paft.

3. *David* when he removed the Ark from
Kirjathjearim, had the Ark put into a new Cart,
which fhould have been carried by the *Koha-
thites. Numb.* 3. 31. And *David* thought this was
right, until the Lord flew *Uzza* for touching
the Ark : But then he looked more exactly into

to the will of God ; and confesseth that the
Lord made a breach upon them, because they
sought him not after the due order, 1 *Chron.*13.
5,7,9,10. & 15. 11, 12, 13. Had not the Lord
made that breach upon them, they had persist-
ed securely in their error.   So I may say in this
case.   In the prosecution of Witchcraft, we
sought not the Lord after the due order; but
have proceeded after the methods used in former times and other places, until the Lord in
this tremendous way made a breach upon us.
And hereby we are made sensible that the methods formerly used are not sufficient to prove
the guilt of such a crime.   And this I conceive
was one end of the Lords letting Satan loose to
torment and accuse so many ; that hereby we
may search out the truth more exactly.   For
had it not been for this dreadful dispensation,
many would have lived and dyed in that error, which they are now convinced of.

  4. The Lord delivered into the hand of Satan, the Estate, Children, and Body of *Job*, for
the tryal of *Jobs* faith and patience, and proof
of his perfection and uprightness.   So the Lord
hath delivered into Satans hand mens Children
and Bodies, yea names and estates into Satans
hand for the tryal of their faith and patience,
and farther manifestation of the sincerity of
their professions.

  7. From that part of the discourse which
shews the power of Satan to torment the bodies,

dies, and disturb the minds of those, he is let
loose upon, *Chap. 6.* I would infer, that Satan
may be suffered so to darken the minds of some
pious Souls, as to cause them to destroy themselves by drowning, hanging, or the like. And
when he hath so far prevailed upon some, that
formerly lived a Christian life, but were under
the prevalency of a distracting Melancholy at
their latter end : We may have Charity that
their Souls are Saved, notwithstanding the sad
conclusion of their lives. I speak not to excuse
any that having the free use of their reason
willingly destroy themselves, out of pride, discontent, impatience, &c. *Achitophel* who out
of heigth of Spirit because his Counsel was not
followed, and to prevent *Davids* executing of
him, for his rebellion, and treason, destroyed
himself, hath left his name to stink unto all ge-
nerations. And *Judas* who for his unparalelled
treachery in betraying his Master, and the
Lord of life, was justly left to hange himself ;
and the rope breaking or slipping he fell down
head long, or with his face down-ward, so that
he burst asunder in the midst, and all his bowels
gushed out, *Matth. 27. 5. with Aξ. 1. 18.* left by
his sin and punishment in the last act of his life
the black character of a Son of perdition. But
those that being out of their right minds, and
hurried by an evil Spirit, as persons under a
force to be their own executioners, are not always to be ranked with these.

8. Seeing

8. Seeing we have been too fierce againſt
ſuppoſed *Malefick* Witchcraft; let us take heed
we do not on the contrary become too favoura-
ble to divining Witchcraft : And become like
Saul who was too zealous againſt the *Gibeonites*,
and at laſt turned to ſeek after one that had a
familiar Spirit, to his own deſtruction. Let us
not, if we can help it, ſuffer Satan to ſet up an
enſuring office for ſtolen Goods. That after
he hath brought the curſe of God into the houſe
of the thief, by tempting him to ſteal : he
may not bring about the curſe into the houſes
of them from whom the goods were ſtolen ;
by alluring them to go to the god of *Ekron* to
enquire. That men may not give their Souls
to the Devil in exchange, for his reſtoring to
them their goods again, in ſuch a way of divination. The Lord grant it may be ſaid of
New England, as is prophecyed of *Judah*, *Mic.*
5. 12. *I will cut off Witchcrafts out of thine hand,
and thou ſhalt have no more ſoothſayers.*

9. Another extream we muſt beware of, is,
viz. Becauſe our fathers in the beginning times
of this Land, did not ſee ſo far into theſe myſ-
teries of iniquity, as hath been ſince diſcovered.
Let us not undervalue the good foundations
they laid for God and his people, and for us
in Church and Civil Government. For *Paul*
that eminent Apoſtle knew but in part ; no
wonder then, if our Fathers were imperfect
men. In the pureſt times in *Iſrael*, there were
                                        ſome

some Clouds of ignorance over-shadowing of
them. *Abraham, David,* and the best Patri-
archs were generally ignorant of the sin of
Polygamy. And although *Solomon* far exceed-
ed *Nehemiah* in wisdom; yet *Nehemiah* saw
farther into the evil of Marrying Outlandish
Women, than that wisest of Kings, and other
fallen men. *Neh.* 13. 26. *Josiah* kept the Passe-
over more exactly, than *David,* and all the
Reforming Kings of *Judah,* 2 *Chron.* 35. 18.

All the godly Judges and Kings of *Judah*
were unacquainted with, and so negligent of
the right observation of the feast of Taberna-
cles, until it came to *Nehemiahs* time: And he
understood and revived an ordinance of God,
that lay buried in oblivion, near about a thou-
sand years. Now he that shall reject all the
good in doctrine and practice, which was main-
tained, professed and practiced by so many
Godly leaders, because of some few errors
found among them, will be found to fight a-
gainst God. A dwarf upon a giants shoulders,
can see farther than the giant.

It was a glorious enterprize of the beginners
of these Colonies, to leave their native Country
to propagate the Gospel : And a very high
pitch of faith, zeal, and courage that carryed
them forth, to follow the Lord into this wilderness, into a land that was not sown. Then
was *New England* holiness to the Lord, and all
that did devour them, or attempted so to do, did
offend

offend, and evil did come upon them. *And the Lord did graciously remember this kindness of their Youth, and love of their Espousals ;.* In granting them many eminent tokens of his favour ; by his presence with them in his Ordinances, for the Conversion of Souls, and edifying and comforting the hearts of his Servants : By signal answering their prayers in times of difficulty : By protecting them from their Enemies : By guiding of, and providing for them in a Desart. And the Lord will still remember this their kindness unto their Posterity, unless that by their Apostasy from the Lord, they vex his Holy Spirit, to turn to be their Enemy : And thereby cut off the Entail of his Covenant Mercies ; which God forbid. *Oh that the Lord may be with us, as he was with our Fathers ; and that he may not leave us, nor forsake us !*

F I N I S.